SOUND-

-ADVICE

SOUND-
-ADVICE

Michael Combatti

Pittsburgh, PA

ISBN 1-56315-245-2

Trade Paperback
© Copyright 2001 Michael Combatti
All rights reserved
First Printing—2001
Library of Congress #00-110570

Request for information should be addressed to:

SterlingHouse Publisher, Inc.
The Sterling Building
440 Friday Road
Pittsburgh, PA 15209
www.sterlinghousepublisher.com

Cover design: Michelle Lenkner - SterlingHouse Publisher, Inc.
Book Designer: N.J. McBeth

Printed in the United States of America

Introduction:

The pleasure is all mine...

If you're anything like me you've probably already skipped over this introduction. However, on the outside chance you're giving it the once over, I thought you might be interested to learn that discovering the **choice concept** and recognizing the power of **sound-advice** came at an ideal time in my life. I'd recently achieved headliner status in the world of stand up comedy; along with the title, I found myself performing in some pretty exotic places and having a bit of success. I was also becoming just a tad filled with myself. I plainly needed what some people regard as an attitude adjustment. As it turned out, I not only created an easy way to adjust my attitude, but in the process I was able to design a simple strategy for positive change.

The choice concept rocked my world and shocked my senses. For the first time in my life I had a plan; one that demanded that I no longer suspend my success. Sound-advice became the blueprint I used to turn my dreams into reality. Weight loss was only the beginning of that dream, then a loving relationship, and finally something that I was convinced only happened to other people, (money *-real money*.)

Virginia Woolf, the world renowned English novelist said that few people ask from books what books can give them. She stated that most commonly we come to books with blurred and divided minds, asking of fiction that it shall be true, of poetry that it shall be false, of biography that it shall be flattering, and that history shall enforce our own prejudices. "Banish all such preconceptions when you read," she said. "Become the author," she announced. "Be his fellow worker and accomplice. If you hang back, and reserve and criticize at first, you are preventing yourself from getting the fullest possible value from what you read. But if you open your mind as widely as possible, then signs and hints of almost imperceptible fineness, from the twist and turn of the first sentences, will bring you into the presence of a human being unlike any other." Embrace Virginia's **sound-advice**. Place your preconceptions on hold. Give *Self-Help* your undivided attention and I guarantee you'll race toward your dreams.

Michael Combatti

This book is dedicated to
anyone I ever met who is
drawing breath, and quite
a few who aren't...

When I was born, I was so surprised I couldn't talk for a year and a half...

Gracie Allen

Choices

I was lying on the sofa in my aunt and uncle's Boca Raton home shortly before Hurricane Andrew wreaked havoc on Southern Florida. Temperatures across the sunshine state were soaring while I continued to maintain a prone position in the family room with the air conditioner cranked up to arctic high. Inside it was *The Ice-Man Cometh* while outside squirrels were placing ice cubes under their nuts.

I was cooling my heals in Boca before heading down to a comedy club in Key West, a sensational room I'd headlined in the past, and if the comedy gods were looking upon me favorably it would be another killer week in the Florida Keys. After working the Keys, I was off to Puerto Rico and the Grand Cayman Islands; eight weeks later the tour would wind up on St. Thomas. Working in the Caribbean was a dirty job but someone had to do it.

Working as a stand-up comic in the tropical islands was always a kick, but I thoroughly enjoyed Florida as well, especially since I got the opportunity to spend time with my aunt and uncle. I especially enjoyed my stay with my relatives because after my visit I'd generally have another ten minutes for my act —Faye and Louie tell it like it is. Teddy Roosevelt's daughter Alice Longworth, an outspoken Washington socialite, once said, "If you haven't got anything nice to say about anyone, come and sit here by me." Teddy's daughter would have adored my Uncle Louie and Aunt Faye, two feisty New Yorkers commonly called *Snowbirds* by the locals. They're Brooklynites who live in Florida during the winter months then soar back to their northern nests for the summer solstice. This summer however, before spreading their wings for the Big Apple, they gave me the keys to their home and said *mi casa es su casa* —a very loving gesture.

Moments before my aunt and uncle took to the road in their Chevy Impala, loaded with bags of juicy oranges for their neighbors in Brooklyn, my uncle, a tall muscular man with jet black hair and horn rimmed glasses, turned to me and said, "I know it's a long shot, but if you get lucky, make sure our neighbors get an eyeful. The frosties around here could use a little excitement."

Uncle Louie frequently referred to his elderly peers as "frosties," alluding to their gray hair or lack thereof. Only a week earlier, I was running some errands with Louie, when he spied an elderly woman in the car ahead of us and announced, "Look there's a giant cotton ball with two arms driving a Lincoln!" I've always suspected that some portion of my own wacky sense of humor, might easily be attributed to my Uncle Louis. Of course, if you ask my uncle, I'm certain he'd readily deny it.

With a broad smile, I handed Louie the last sack of oranges and said, "Superman, if I get lucky, I'll send your neighbors the video."

Superman is a term of endearment my cousins and I often use whenever we address our uncle, a moniker that originated in the fifties when every kid in the Fort Green projects was convinced that my uncle was none other than Clark Kent. The mild mannered reporter, who fought for truth, justice, and the American way. Just for the record, I'm certain the rumor about his "secret identity" was started by Uncle Louie. When my uncle cracked his frosty joke, my mother's older sister Filippa (everyone calls her Faye) just shook her head, rolled her eyes and waved good-bye. Of course, before the burgundy Chevy could make a clean get away, Aunt Faye shouted from the passenger window, "Don't forget to eat the sausage and peppers in the freezer!" Italians, you gotta love 'em.

Later that same day, I was sprawled out in the family room, a bag of Doritos propped up between my legs, the remote control in one hand and a Bud Light in the other. I was sippin', snackin' and surfin' when I finally dropped anchor on an afternoon talk show. I couldn't tell you if it was Sally, Ricki or Oprah, however I am certain of one thing. The moment I logged on, a beautiful woman looked directly into the camera and changed my life forever. After a long pause and a broad smile that went from one corner of the television set to the other, she announced, "I finally understand that I always have a choice."

It appeared that she'd recently lost a great deal of weight and that simple realization had saved her life. At that moment, this beautiful woman through her head back and laughed, and then she said, "I lost a whole 'nother person." She was honest and straightforward and I believed her when she announced that for the first time in her life she truly understood the power of choice; something she had never seriously contemplated and neither had I.

I switched off the television, but I could still hear that pleasing women's voice, affirming, "I finally understand that I always have a choice." It was a simple statement that went straight to my heart. I repeated it again and again, then I began to think about the actual concept of choice, and how I might apply it to my life. Could I choose to be healthier, wealthier and even more compassionate? The answer was a resounding YES. The more choice questions I asked, the more yes answers I received. With each affirmative response I collected, I became more excited. I felt like a cartoon character with a light bulb appearing above my head. All at once I was peaceful, yet giddy. Then, as if I were listening to a voice other than my own, I proclaimed out loud, "I always have a choice." I'd had an awakening, a bright moment in which I understood what Ebineezer Scrooge experienced when he awoke on Christmas morning. It was a visitation of my own spirit past, present and future. Mr. Scrooge recognized that he had a second chance and now so did I. It was the forest for the trees, the coffee brewing and the aroma of the roses I hadn't stopped to smell. I got it. But what had I gotten? What was it that I finally understood? After all, I'd learned freedom of choice about the same time children were bustling around Uncle Louie shouting Superman. What was it that had me towering above the clouds and grinning from ear to ear?

My exhilaration and new found awareness was a concept I dubbed the choice concept and sound-advice. Positive recurring messages I continuously use to orchestrate the best possible attitude. I was about to create a sequence of instant reminders prompting and challenging my decision making powers from one moment to the next. The sound of my own voice, often spoken out loud, gave me the power to drive the right choice home at the right time. I understood something I'd known all my life, but now I was seeing it in a new way. After all, that's what learning was all about.

At first it seemed too simple, but directly the choice concept and sound-advice proved to be undeniable —it clearly worked. In truth, attending to sound-advice not only worked, it was highly effective. My friend on the talk show recognized it; she knew that she had to control her choices from one moment to another. She determined that in order to change her eating habits, she'd have to recall the moment of truth on demand. Pledges that quickly announced that the power of choice was always there for the asking.

At last, I found the key I'd dropped down a storm drain, years earlier. Since then, it had been a little overcast. However, now the sun was breaking through the clouds, and off in the distance a rainbow revealed a treasure chest, yearning to be unlocked. It was an essential piece to a puzzle I'd misplaced or perhaps chose to disregard. Instantly, my feet were firmly planted in the moment. I knew that I could do anything my heart desired. I could choose to accept love unconditionally and give love unconditionally. At once I understood that by living in the moment and utilizing sound-advice life could be lived to the fullest.

The choice concept had enormous strength, although I still had to find a way to harness that energy. I had to develop a workable program in which to effect the innocent reminders I called sound-advice, tribute as it were from my next breath to my last.

Repetition quickly became the nucleus for my sound-advice incantations. Allowing my conscious mind to repeat admonitions at will, may have been the most important discovery of my life. I learned to accept a stream of consciousness that served to push procrastination out the window. Once and for all, the time had come to stop delaying my own success. Now, every day was about to become Independence Day. However, in order to make my dreams materialize, I'd have to vigorously exercise my physical, as well as my emotional muscles. Choosing to surf aimlessly with my life on remote control was out. My choices would be mine only if I owned them lock, stock and barrel.

Always listen to experts.
They'll tell you what
can't be done and why.
Then do it...

Robert Heinlein

Sound-Advice

When the concept of **sound-advice** stirred my heart, I was like a kid in a candy shop. Oddly enough, not unlike my friend on the talk show, candy shops were some of my favorite haunts. In fact, a modification on an old joke might go "If you look up the word **sweet-tooth** in the dictionary, you're likely to find my photograph next to the word with my mouth ajar, pointing to a lower bicuspid." However, let me not lead you astray. I not only crave sweets, no no my friends, I simply love to eat; feed, feast, graze, have a picnic, throw a clambake... excuse me, could you please pass the gravy?

I recall one foggy Christmas eve, just after a comic friend and I had brought a little humor to the wealthy, we decided to drive over to our favorite twenty-four hour, five-star restaurant, Ché Denny's. We were a few hours late for the traditional midnight snack, but for us, that was just a mere technicality.

By the time I'd finished giving the waitress my order —only seconds before her eyes had completely glazed over— my comic companion turned to me and said, "Mikie, I think you may have an eating disorder you eat **dis** order, you eat **dat** order." Obviously the joke was on me, especially since my amusing friend resembled a condominium with legs and therefore knew a *true* fellow chubster when he saw one.

There was no denying that my comic colleague had hit the proverbial nail on the head. I not only ate like a man on a mission, I ate like a bull elephant on a mission. When the dinner bell sounded, I was the guy on the porch banging the triangle. If you heard my name called twice while waiting for a table at a restaurant, doubtless I'd expired. However, now I'd discovered something far better than the Colonel's seven spices, or a warehouse brimming with secret sauce. I'd found the absolute power of choice. The ability to recognize the authority of my own voice. I'd simply found a unique means of hearing my own **sound-advice**. By utilizing a simple diversion, I discovered a way to unlock my daily feeding frenzy. It was a word game —a sound vibration I no longer chose to ignore. I dubbed my simple device "the appetizer alternative," an admonition I use at home, or while dining at an eloquent restaurant. I simply say: "Yo, fat-stuff, you have a choice!" However, most of the time I leave off the "Yo" part and on occasion I may even kick out "fat-stuff." Nevertheless, whenever I eat anything, I always remember to give myself a **sound-advice** alert. Does it always work? Frankly, no, it doesn't always work, but damned if it doesn't slap me across the teeth often enough to make a difference. I announce my appetizer alternative aloud, making it difficult for me to hide behind the silent agreement I have to eat more food than I require. It's a **sound**-system that reminds me that I'm not on death row, so whatever I'm eating, probably won't be my last meal. Certainly it's a tad wacky, but it's just wacky enough to compel me to slow down and eat less.

When I accepted the concept of **sound-advice**, the first extraordinary thing that occurred was a foolproof method for shedding unwanted pounds. At last, I understood that **discipline** wasn't a dirty word. I had two choices. I could continue to use lip-service with regard to shaking up my world, or I could get my behind in gear. I began swimming every day. Excuses, such as "limited time" and various other reasons I invented to maintain an unhealthy state, such as, "I'm too tired," or "I'm too busy," were no longer effectual. Instead, I chose to make the time I needed to get healthy and stay healthy. I had to do it for me. I had to define the man I wanted to be. I swam for an hour a day, talking out loud as I lifted my head out of the water. Sometimes, I'd swallow a mouth-full; however, I still continued to tell myself that I would never be fat again. In fact, those were often the exact words I used, "I'll never be fat again, glug, glug, gurgle, gurgle." I no longer wished to be in denial. Besides, who was I kidding, if I turned my head around and looked in the mirror, I saw a butt the size of Cleveland. If I bent over to put a blanket down on the sand at the beach, I'd block out the sun. So, I chose to exercise a minimum of an hour a day for six months without fail; a feat I'd never done before. If I wasn't swimming, I was riding an exercise bicycle or jogging. But, whatever exercise I was doing, I was always talking out loud. It didn't matter if anyone heard me barking out an aphorism like, "I'm healthy, wealthy and wise," while I was running. It was of no consequence to me if anyone thought I was a nutball or a guy on a cell phone. I was using **sound-advice** to keep myself honest and damned if it wasn't working. The bottom line is that as long as I continue to use the appetizer alternative, and listen to **sound-advice**, while I exercise every day, I'm able to wear pants that make me look and feel more like a man than a wounded wildebeest.

Sound-advice not only took the weight off, but it continues to keep it off. My simple formula was simply designing a better me; however, weight loss was just the first step on my journey toward acquiring a better attitude. Now every time I climbed on stage, I wasn't learning about who I was, but rather who I was capable of becoming. My **sound-advice** alert gradually became my mantra, conveying comfort while options unfolded from one moment to the next. I began counseling and cautioning myself on a moment's notice, which not only gave me the strength to choose between fat and thin, but also the power to choose between sharing and not sharing or caring and not caring. It felt as if a gigantic snowball was barreling uphill and gaining momentum, eager to crush prehistoric fear and perch atop a mountain of success. Sound vibrations and instantaneous reflections were about to change my decision-making process forever. I practiced the **sound-advice** system, until I became it and it became me. I was attending to an echo that sounded like a quiet thunder. I was listening to a healthy voice resonating a healthy choice. Moreover, I'd arrived at something innocent and spontaneous, not just a pie in the sky fiasco.

The choice concept was more than just the luck of the draw, it was money in the bank. I'd no sooner gamble with my future, than would I expect a software engineer to fashion a computer out of spam. I made the choice to listen intently to my **sound** alert system. Inspired, I now had the ability to cause an avalanche of achievement. My intentions were crystal clear, it was easy to identify my goals. I accomplished my objectives by no longer pretending to be in the moment. I was either there or I wasn't.

So, now it was time to combine previous lessons with **sound-advice** techniques; principles I was destined to view in a new way. I was ready to recall the past, pay attention to the present and look toward the future.

The distance
doesn't matter; only the
first step is difficult...

Mme. du Deffand

Risky Business

Frankie Farrell was giving me a lift home on his Columbia bicycle since it was nearly dinner time and I'd had a serious lapse in judgment, considering my mother would be just a wee bit irritable whenever I arrived home a tad late. Besides, *The Three Stooges* with Officer Joe Bolton, the master of ceremonies, was must see T.V. at five o'clock, and I wasn't about to miss one slap, crackle, or pop performed by the Horowitz brothers and Larry Fine.

Frankie and I had been hanging out at the handball courts in Marine Park, hitting on the girls from our fifth grade class, running around like crazy people and on occasion, playing a game or two of handball. I'd walked to the park that day so when Frankie said he was heading home, I asked him if I might catch a ride on his Columbia. Naturally, he wasn't thrilled with the idea. However, Frankie held fast to his handlebars and with his feet firmly planted on the sidewalk, he said "Climb on."

I was sitting on the frame wedged between Frankie and the handlebars, a snug fit even though Columbia bicycles had the thickest frame of any bike on the market. Columbia bicycles also had massive fenders with wide tires and a horn that was almost as irritating as Fran Dresher's voice, not to mention a headlight that could easily illuminate an airport runway. In truth, if you melt down a Columbia bicycle you can build two Isuzu Rodeos and a Lincoln Terminator and you'd still have enough metal left over for a nifty bicycle-rack. Frankie definitely had his work cut out for him, considering that whenever I needed new pants, my mom's choices were limited to the husky boys rack at the Robert Hall's department store.

We were going along at a pretty good clip until my chauffeur hit a serious incline. Frankie was giving it everything he had, when all at once it felt as if we were doing a scene from a Sam Peckinpah movie and everything appeared to be moving in slow motion.

At that moment I turned toward Frankie and said, "We're moving so slowly I think we're actually going backwards. Look, a snail is passing us on the right!" Martin & Lewis were comedy kings in those days and Uncle Miltie was clearing millions for the Texaco oil cartel, but that afternoon as far as Frankie Farrell was concerned his pal Mikie ruled the roost.

Frankie generally thought my one liners were pretty funny, but that one put him over the top. Apparently it was the funniest thing he'd ever heard, because he fell off his bike and rolled around on the ground laughing for a full minute.

When Frankie regained his composure he affirmed, "When you say funny stuff it takes my strength away, so try not to be too funny or you'll have to walk home."

Of course I continued to say funny stuff, and although sapped of his strength, Frankie still took me all the way home.

The following day I arrived at the Good Shepherd school yard while Frankie was telling some of our friends about our little bicycle trip. I was approaching the small gathering, when I heard Frankie say, "A snail get it ?! Don't ya get it 'a snail'!" His audience seemed to think the story was mildly amusing. However, had Frankie known the phrase "I guess you just had to be there," I'm certain he would have used it in a heartbeat. I sensed that Frankie was losing the audience, so I chimed in and told them how funny Frankie looked when he was rolling around on the ground. I said that he looked like a flounder flappin' on the deck of a fishing boat in Sheepshead Bay. In a flash, I was down on the ground recreating the moment. I had them laughing their eleven-year-old butts off until the school bell rang and it was time to stop clowning around in the school yard and continue clowning around in the classroom. Before the guards, I mean the nuns, could swoop down on us and ruin a great moment, Frankie smiled at me and extended his hand and we quickly took our place in line.

Then our class began filing through the huge oak doors and up the slate stairs to our overcrowded classrooms, where to this day it remains a mystery how I ever learned anything. In truth, if the Dominican nuns had given out grades for staring out the window, I would have received straight As. Or had the good sisters offered praise for the best farm animal sound effects, I may have topped the honor role eight years in a row.

So of course it had to be destiny years later when I decided to test the waters during stand-up comedy's rock of the eighties. After all, I could make Frankie Farrell fall off his bicycle after listening to my snappy repartee. And I could still do a pretty good impression of a fish flappin' on the deck of a boat. Besides, now I was a foot taller and *joke boy* at all the parties, so why not bring my special brand of humor to the stage. In addition, I'd seen Robin Williams at *The Holy City Zoo* in San Francisco, performing his rapid fire routine, long before anyone knew who he was and he made stand-up comedy look easy. However, I soon learned that making friends laugh at parties and getting an audience to give up the guffaws on cue was a horse of a different color.

When I arrived at *The Other Café* in the Haight-Ashbury district, I was more panicky than a plump turkey on a pilgrim's chopping block. I'd finally summoned the nerve to sign up for my first open-mike comedy night and I was terrified. All the comics had butterflies in their stomachs while I had flying monkeys playing hard ball in mine. I was beyond nervousness; I'd clearly pushed the outside of the envelope and was approaching acute anxiety. I was convinced that as soon as I climbed on stage I wouldn't be able to remember one funny story or a single solitary joke. So before I arrived that evening, I recorded all my skits and sketches on a tiny tape recorder and placed the small recorder down my pants. I snaked the tiny recorder's earplug through my shorts, under my shirt and into my left ear. Then, I concealed the entire affair with a wacky wig and a big floppy hat. I thought that if I got on stage and my mind went blank, unable to recall my three minutes of prepared hilarity, I could listen to my little electronic friend in my trousers and all would be well again. Pretty ingenious, except I was so nervous I accidentally pulled the tape recorder plug out of the socket as soon as I stepped up to the microphone. I'd not only lost my electronic adviser, but now I had the sound of my own muffled voice telling jokes from my crotch. I immediately tried to speak louder than my crotch, but I couldn't remember anything I'd prepared, so I was basically screwed.

Comics commonly refer to that kind of experience as *eating it, big time*. One might say that I went down like the Hindenberg landing on the Titanic. The audience just stared at me like trout. I'm sure they thought I'd planned the muffled voice from the pants routine, but weren't certain why anyone might think that was particularly funny. When the red light informing me that my time on stage was up I announced, "Thank 'God' my time is up," while a heckler from the audience proclaimed "Amen."

The following afternoon over lunch I told my friend Samantha about my first experience with stand-up comedy and that I wanted to avoid taking any further risks. Samantha said that she felt that that was a dangerous thing to do. "Give it another shot," she said. "If you fail to confront your fears, they may become your best friends or your worst nightmares." Samantha had been an actress with the Shakespearean Repertory Theater in Boston for quite a few years and clearly understood the meaning of the word *risk*. We talked a bit more about stage fright and then she suggested a piece of advice that would forever reverberate in my ears.

Samantha said, "Why don't you invite your fear to attend your next open-mike performance. Tell your fear to sit right up front and enjoy the show."

A funny notion and perhaps an abstract image, but the message was crystal clear.

A few days later I used Samantha's idea and it made a world of difference. I was still nervous, but something wonderful happened in the process. I understood that if I put my fear aside and recalled Samantha's **sound-advice** whenever I needed it, I could do anything, even stand-up comedy. Gradually, stage fright became a distant memory and a few years later I was headlining comedy clubs from Vancouver to the Virgin Islands.

I listened to **sound-advice** and challenged my fear to a duel and I won. Now I challenge mediocrity more than I ever have in the past. I dare myself to choose the right path and I defy anyone to stop me. Not unlike my work on stage, I've learned to invite routine doubts and fears to take a front row seat and witness the magic.

Winston Churchill once said, "We have nothing to fear except fear itself." I use Sir Winston's aphorism to remind myself that fear keeps me motionless, that if I choose not to be ruled by my emotions and never to be fearful of taking risks, I'll regularly achieve success. Presently those reminders have become an integral part of the sound vibrations I pay heed to on a moment's notice, that inner voice that recalls Samantha's little trick whenever doubt or fear rears its ugly head, or when I space out for a moment and forget that I always have a choice.

Whenever I travel to New York, invariably I'm drawn to the old neighborhood. Before I can say, "Moe, Larry and Curly," I find myself standing by the handball courts in Marine Park, glancing at the faces of the passersby in hopes that I'll recognize an old friend. Thus far, no luck, but I'll be back soon and who knows I may even run into my old handball partner Frankie Farrell. In a perfect world Frankie will announce that he read my book and that he frequently practices **sound-advice**. Of course in an even more perfect world he'd come tooling by on his old Columbia bicycle, which in today's market would be worth a small fortune. Then, Frankie would tell me a story that loses something in the translation. However, with a little luck, when that happened Frankie would quickly announce, "I guess you just had to be there."

Tomorrow doesn't matter for I have lived today...

Horace

The optimist proclaims
that we live in the best
of all possible worlds,
and the pessimist fears
this is true...

James Branch Cabell

Beaches, Blankets
and Babylon

In the early eighties I had the good fortune to work for the late great Steve Silver. Mr. Silver created the highly successful San Francisco musical comedy Beach Blanket Babylon. Complete with towering hats the size of Buicks and bursting with contemporary music and current crazes, *BBB* promised a zany evening at the theater. Although I didn't sing or dance on the stage of the Fugazi Theater, I still wore several hats —one as the house manager and the other working behind the scenes as a stagehand. Two minutes before the curtain would rise, I'd exchange my bellboy attire —complete with pork pie hat- for a sweat shirt and jeans. Then, I'd slip backstage and work alongside some of the best singers, dancers and comedic actors in the business to create the magic tourists and natives alike have enjoyed for over a quarter of a century.

On occasion I'd earn a couple of extra dollars by walking around the streets of San

Francisco dressed like a giant peanut, that's PEANUT just in case you're speed reading. A nine foot plastic Mr. Peanut costume complete with green tights and leprechaun-bootie attachments, that gingerly slipped over my Reeboks. First I'd hit every street in North Beach, annoying the locals at the outdoor cafes and the store owners in nearby Chinatown, then I'd waddle my way over to Union Square in search of the out-of-towners. Soon after, I'd cruise down to Fisherman's Wharf, pausing along the way to tell anyone within earshot that I was absolutely "nuts" about my job. As soon as I had someone's undivided attention, I might even mention the show at the Fugazi Theater.

Steve made certain that I pounded the pavement whenever his writers created a new motif for the show, which usually coincided with current trends and passing fads. Naturally, whenever the theme of the show changed, the musical comedy's title would have to be modified. When surf boarding films like *Blue Hawaii* and songs like *Little Surfer Girl* by the Beach Boys were at their peak, Steve Silver deposited tons of sand and sea shells in every nook and cranny of the theater. The staff was dressed in bathing suits and flip-flops, and the show was called, **Beach Blanket Babylon goes to the Beach.**

Then, one glorious morning, I opened the *San Francisco Chronicle* and turned to the theater section, where I was delighted to read,

Beach Blanket Babylon Goes to Washington.

When I arrived at the theater that afternoon, Steve Silver asked me to take to the streets in my wacky peanut suit to promote our good fortune. He said that the entire cast and crew would be traveling to the nation's capitol to perform for the President and the First Lady.

For the next few weeks, I walked along the streets of San Francisco in my peanut apparel, proclaiming that I would soon be lunching with the president of the free world and his wife. (I'm certain everyone I encountered took me at my word). When I called my mom to tell her the exciting news, I mentioned the photo opportunities I'd have at the White House. The following day my mother purchased a silver picture frame for the 8x10 glossy that would soon grace her living room wall. My parents would soon be uttering the words, "That's my son standing between Ron and Nancy. No, it's not trick photography. He's in show business."

I couldn't help but feel a tinge of hypocrisy laced with my new found enthusiasm, especially since I frequently proclaimed that whenever the President spoke, it looked as though his entire head was likely to start spinning around. I'd also voiced an opinion or two concerning Ronald's "acting" ability. Frankly, I always thought Ronny was a much better actor in Washington than he'd ever been in Hollywood. It was still pretty exciting stuff for a boy from the south (South Brooklyn) living in Berkeley, California traveling to our nation's capitol to do an off-Broadway production of the most bastardized version of *Snow White and the Seven Dwarfs* anyone could ever imagine.

Preparations for the gala event were made months in advance, airline reservations and hotel accommodations were arranged while the prop makers worked overtime on the leading lady's grand finale hat; a hat the size of Cleveland...make that Washington. A forty-three pound hat with extended shoulder braces cleverly concealed under the actor's costume. It was a giant rotating hat with a miniature District of Columbia atop and the Washington Monument thrown in for good measure, which during the final crowd pleasing song rises —one can only imagine— from the depths of the leading lady's brain. Frankly, wherever the monolith was ascending from was certain to stop the show. Unfortunately, that hat-trick and a plethora of others would never be seen by the President and his wife, inasmuch as shortly before we were to take to the air our command performance was stamped null and void. Like water in a paper sack, the bottom had fallen out of our presidential presentation and we were left holding the bag.

The cancellation had something to do with our union affiliations or lack thereof, and some other psycho-babble about political ramifications during an election year. None of it made any sense, but whether the umpire needed contact lenses or not, we were all out at the plate. Everyone connected with the show walked around wearing the same face; the "I can't believe I'm not going to perform at the White House" face. But before we could take our victim routine too far, a bizarre spectacle began to take shape all around us. Steve Silver began making preparations to throw the wildest party any of us had ever witnessed. The entire affair was catered with an assortment of exotic foods and beverages; lobsters from Maine, conch from the Cayman Islands, caviar from...wherever caviar comes from when it's very expensive. Imported wines were flowing like so much bottled water, while celebs and friends of the show flew in from all over the country. There were more talented people at the Fugazi Theater than the Dorothy Chandler Pavilion had for the recent Academy Awards. As luck would have it, before anyone could say "That's entertainment!" the guests and the performers from *B B B* were putting on the best variety show since Ed Sullivan presented the Beatles. Beside the dancing bear, the only act missing was the guy who twirls dinner plates on long pointed sticks. In fact, the sea lions balancing beach balls were on just before the Rockettes. The show was so long I thought I was watching the Jerry Lewis Telethon. The show's gifted musicians started jamming and didn't stop until the sunrise splashed across the bay and through the keyholes of the black lacquered theater doors.

Steve's powerful message seemed at first a little crazy, but gradually I understood that he was crazy like a fox. We were celebrating the present, rather than dwelling on what might have been in the future. Choosing to focus on the positive things in his life, Mr. Silver surrounded himself with people who live their lives in the moment. He recognized the malady, acknowledged the extent of the damage and moved on. Steve Silver was a man who took responsibility for his life and his lifestyle.

I continue to exercise my personal brand of guidance while recalling the **sound-advice** I often received from Steve Silver. It's a game that sends up a flare anytime misleading or self-serving behavior makes an appearance. I took something precious away with me when I left the employ of *Beach Blanket Babylon*. I left with the understanding that living in the moment works best when I share it; that not unlike grasping a foreign language, **the choice concept** and **sound-advice** are easily understood when I practice the fundamental principles with others. The world renowned essayist and poet Ralph Waldo Emerson said, "There is guidance for each of us, and by lowly listening, we shall hear the right word." I acknowledge his affirmation by quietly listening to my inner voice and recognizing that the sounds of success may sometimes come from elf-like shoes pounding the pavement or from the innocence of my youth.

When Steve Silver was making preparations for his outrageous soiree, I asked him why he was throwing a party and he said, "Nikita Khrushchev once said, 'Life is short. Live it up.' " Then Steve smiled and walked away. The lessons I learned from Steve Silver and the spontaneity he often demonstrated reminds me to embrace life from one moment to the next. It's that childlike naiveté which allows me to say what I mean and mean what I say. Recalling **sound-advice** compels me to picture my abilities, not my disabilities, while my inner voice urges me to replace uncertainty with confidence and indecision with independence. When I stay in the moment, I'm at the controls of a fine tooled machine. A vehicle with strength and agility highly polished to a cool green brilliance, the color of money. It's a formidable formula that has become my ticket to ride. And, as long as I pay attention to the moment, I'll continue to cruise down the highway with the top down and a pair of elf-like booties hanging from the rear view mirror.

Our true age can be determined by the ways in which we allow ourselves to play...

Louis Walsh

When you have eliminated the impossible, whatever remains is the truth...

Arthur Conan Doyle

Questions and Answers

I was stuck in traffic when I spied an archaic bumper sticker on an even more archaic Volkswagen Mini-bus. The bumper sticker announced: *Question Authority!* Naturally, the first thing that popped into my fertile imagination was how cool it would be to view that manifesto on the bumper of a police cruiser. Dollars to donuts that'll never happen, but it's the thought that counts. In case anyone's keeping score, placing the word *police* adjacent to a sentence containing the word *donuts* was purely coincidental.

Moments later, in a cloud of dust, the mini-bus with the proclamation stapled to the wooden bumper exited the freeway. No sooner had my counter-revolutionary friend taken his leave, when the lane to my right parted like the Red Sea and I was on my way. Or at least as "on my way" as anyone traveling the freeways surrounding the city of San Francisco can be. Still, I pointed my car toward home and began thinking about creating my own bumper sticker. That's when the phrase *question commitment* popped into my head —it'd been a long commute.

In truth, only a few months had past since I began paying tribute to **the choice concept** and effecting **sound-advice**. Nevertheless, my new found attitude adjustments were already beginning to empower me. I felt as though I were viewing people from a better place and in turn the general population was witnessing positive changes in yours truly. With each passing day I felt more at ease than I ever had in the past. I'd finally chosen to keep the moment close at hand and assemble the strength I needed to challenge prior beliefs, so naturally my imaginary bumper sticker was a timely reminder.

Toying with the notion to regularly question my commitments was intriguing inasmuch as my self-motivating techniques would no longer allow me to leave well enough alone. Time and again **sound-advice** was proving that well enough wasn't good enough. Granted certain questions made me uncomfortable, but I knew that if I didn't challenge my commitment to my craft or my physical well-being on a regular basis I might run the risk of reverting back to the complacent human being I'd been. In addition, **sound-advice** questions made it difficult to ignore my word or the promises I continually made to myself and than casually abandoned. The self-motivating tools I was using were compelling me to confront my fears and that meant being totally honest with myself before I could be completely candid with others. I knew that without asking myself tough questions, my ego would still dictate the degree of honesty I chose to live by —heightening indecision— and that was no longer an option. So I began jotting down questions I'd been vacillating about for years and I discovered that by viewing honest answers to hard hitting questions —in black and white— I could no longer hide from the truth. I began reading them again and again and just like all the other **sound-advice** techniques I'd been practicing faithfully, once again I was creating another link to better choices. Now every evening after dinner, I read the tough questions I originally wrote down after my initial encounter with the mini-bus. My questions have given me the courage to be my own constructive critic. Questions like: "Am I following my plan to improve my station in life?" And, "Do I try to make myself appear more important than I need to be?"

When I awake in the morning, I extend my regimen by questioning my commitments once again. I challenge my word in the shower and by the time I'm dressed, I'm ready to do battle. I refer to my morning ritual as my daybreak proclamations; sunrise solace that celebrates my life and compels me to operate from a place of sincerity. It's an awakening that offers positive reinforcement, a device that allows me to view the light at the end of the tunnel and the pot of gold at the end of the rainbow. Each morning I remind myself to challenge my intentions, stay focused and remain in the moment. In the moment, I'm likely to view procrastination as a cross I no longer care to carry. In the moment, if I experience guilt, I'm also likely to welcome it for the positive function it plays in my life.

My daily *Q* and *A* program helps me to maintain a constant state of self-motivation — sound bites on a conscious level. However, time and again the data required to maintain my self-motivating spirit was trickling into my unconscious. In truth, a dream I recently had might be considered one part nightmare, two parts revelation. Although the nightmare portion of my illusion may have been the result of a pizza I shared with my wife shortly before we hit the sack —the verdict is still out.

In my stormy dream, I was dressed like the Gorton's fisherman appearing on a packet of fish sticks in the freezer section of my local supermarket. I was standing on the deck of a small fishing boat staring out over the horizon, seemingly unaware of an approaching tsunami. When all at once a giant squall came up like the thunder. However, before I could utter the words: "Hold the anchovies," the colossal wave broke over the bow of the boat and just like Giancarlo Gianini in the classic Lina Wurtmuller film, I was *Swept Away*. Oddly enough, a shipmate who resembled the infamous O.J. Simpson went sailing into the water as well. To add insult to injury, neither I, nor the character that resembled a double murderer knew how to swim. (A bizarre twist inasmuch as I normally swim one hundred laps a day.) Nevertheless, there I was flailing about in rough water, just moments away from sleeping with the fishes. However, I wasn't about to visit Davy Jones' locker without a fight, so I contrived an awkward swimming stroke, kicking and shouting my way toward a dangling rope that had —in true dreamlike fashion— appeared on the port side of the tiny boat. I grasped the rope with both hands and pulled myself aboard. It sounds wacky, I know, but that's how it went down, or rather how I didn't go down. My efforts were rewarded with the breath of life, while my ill-fated shipmate sank like a stone. Poetic justice? Maybe just a tad.

The most vivid component of my stormy ride was that instead of shouting for help I recall crying out: "I've got a choice!" In one split second I took a beat and chose life while the O.J. character allowed death to choose him. When I awoke I didn't remember my scary dream, but later that day —probably while opening a can of tuna— I recalled my illusion and recognized that **sound-advice** was now part of my unconscious. Even in my dreams, I was pausing in the midst of my dilemma while my inner voice was shouting: "You always have a choice!" Come hell or high water, the **choice concept** and **sound-advice** were fashioning unconscious resolutions. Yet, whether conscious or otherwise, my resolve was notably different from any New Year's Eve resolution I'd ever made, considering they frequently vanished before I could say: "Is it the third or fourth of January?"

Although nothing short of outrageous, my wacky dream confirmed that life is often unfair and that we regularly have to wade through an ocean of injustice; however, we still have to risk deep water to be alive —really alive. My wild ride also suggested that being content with strolling through life, rather than purposefully running toward my goals, would no longer work. It also affirmed that I should never trouble to look over my shoulder to see who may be gaining on me. After all, that's none of my concern. **Sound-advice** frequently recalls a classic tune made famous by the late Billy Holiday that announces: "Ain't nobody's business but my own."

So don't be afraid to ask yourself tough questions and ride tsunamis in your dreams. However, just to play it safe, if you're likely to head off to bed soon after your midnight snack, I might suggest having your neighborhood pizzeria hold the anchovies.

The question is laid out
for each of us to ask:
Whether to hold on, or
to drop the mask..

Martha Boesing

I really didn't say
everything I said...

Yogi Berra

Grand Slam

Throughout the summer months in the early sixties, my father and I would take the subway from Coney Island to the Big Apple and beyond. Our journey would shuttle us beneath Flatbush Avenue on a ride that snaked its way across the borough of Brooklyn, only to surface near the East River at the base of the Manhattan Bridge. Occasionally, while the train rattled its way across the bridge, Dad and I would make our way from one subway car to the next, in search of two seats side by side and a breath of fresh air. I recall Dad grasping the handle on the steel door that lead to the platform just outside the moving train, then with a quick jerk he'd slide open the portal, pausing for a split second before crossing the threshold.

At first, stepping outside a moving train in the middle of the Manhattan Bridge fifteen stories above the East River, frequently gave me pause as well. However, the cool breeze above the water and the commanding view from the bridge made it all worthwhile. On one side, the majestic Brooklyn Bridge loomed in the distance. While to the right, the Manhattan skyline from the Empire State Building to Spanish Harlem presented a dramatic backdrop to the most celebrated city in the world. A few minutes later, our train would reach Gotham and quickly disappear below Chinatown and Little Italy, pulling its precious cargo uptown.

In less than an hour, Dad and I were crossing the Harlem River, approaching our final destination —the Bronx and the house that Ruth built. With a baseball glove in one hand and a hot dog with mustard in the other, my father and I would sit in the bleachers with a few thousand other Bronx Bomber fans waiting to snag a long ball hit by the mighty Mickey Mantle or a rocket launched from the bat of the recently dethroned home run king, Roger Maris. Thousands of voices strong, we'd cheer the Yankees and heckle the competition. But win or lose, just being in Yankee Stadium where Babe Ruth and Joe DiMaggio had played the game of baseball was pure ecstasy.

When the contest was over, Dad and I would wend our way down giant ramps, surrounded by a sea of humanity, until we arrived at the turnstiles below the massive entranceway, where a glut of vendors hawking souvenir pennants and baseball hats vied for our attention. Just across the street, I'd race up the same waffled stairway I'd dashed down earlier and stand beside my father on the platform of the elevated train station that ran along 161st Street and River Avenue.

I can still recall punching the pocket of my Little League baseball glove while viewing the massive letters just across the rails that spelled out Yankee Stadium. As the sun disappeared behind the approaching train, a quick glance from my father told me that it was time to stop thumping my mitt and tuck it under my arm. The aging train would usually pull into the subway station like the thunder, rumbling and growling and frequently coming to an abrupt stop, as though a passenger in dire straits had pulled the emergency cord, or perhaps the driver had been admiring the sunset and grabbed the brake handle a tad late, causing the third rail to arc in a hail of sparks while the steel wheels emitted a screeching sound that cut through the orange sky.

As a matter of course, one sliding door on each car would remain hermetically sealed while the remaining door opened at a snail's pace, allowing Dad and I, and what appeared to be the rest of mankind, just enough shoulder room to cram aboard. The lack of space, and occasional elbow thrust to the rib cage, never seemed to be of any consequence. Especially when our New York Yankees were the conquering heroes. Moments later, we were once again crossing the East River into Brooklyn, rounding third and heading home.

Whenever I recall those summer days at Yankee Stadium, I'm frequently reminded of several players I admired. Naturally, like most kids my age, I liked Mantle and Maris, but my personal favorite was Hall of Famer Yogi Berra. Yogi was one of the best catchers the game of baseball has ever produced. He was a brick wall when it came to defending the plate and a powerful batter as well. On or off the playing field, Yogi never failed to shock and amaze, while nearly everything he said brought a smile to my face.

My father often referred to Mr. Berra as "a piece of work," an expression Dad used on occasion when describing an individual he suspected might be two sandwiches short of a picnic. "Yogi's elevator might be stuck between floors," Dad would announce. My father wasn't alone when it came to the Yankee catcher's idiosyncrasies; in truth, Yogi's comments made every baseball fan in America tilt their collective heads to the side. Not unlike a litter of puppies listening to Yoko Ono "sing," or Judge Mills Lane listening to a litigant trying to pull the wool over his eyes.

Nearing the end of the baseball season, when Yogi's contract was nearly up, a newspaper reporter asked him if he knew where he was going. Yogi paused for a second and replied, "If I don't know where I'm going, I might end up somewhere else." Perhaps a tad wacky, yet an affirmation that speaks volumes of a man who had a clear vision of who he was and where he was bound. Yogi Berra knew that if he didn't have a plan, he might have to settle for second best; however, second best wasn't part of his vocabulary. Numero uno was Yogi's mark in trade. It was a quality his legion of fans acknowledged every time the matchless competitor was given the Most Valuable Player Award, a feat he accomplished three times over his colorful career, as well as fourteen pennants and ten World Series Trophies.

When I told my father that I was writing a piece about baseball, Dad mentioned Ebbets Field and a few old timers from the Brooklyn Dodgers. "Duke Snyder and Pee Wee Reese were a couple of warriors," Dad announced. Then, without missing a beat, he added, "But I'll tell ya, that Yank Yogi Berra was a real piece of work." My father said that Yogi was a dangerous hitter and that he knew how to win. Then, my father paused for a second and said, "More importantly, he knew how to lose." Dad was referring to his obvious grace under fire, a winning style rather than a gloating smile. Whenever Yogi Berra was interviewed by the press, he always spoke about the good things he had in his life, making reference to his family and how he regularly looked toward the future. Pretty insightful stuff for a guy who once said, "The game isn't over until the fat lady eats." However, whether the fat lady was eating or singing, Mr.

Berra was and continues to be an original, a paradigm for success.

While he may not always appear mindful of his inventive observations, Yogi Berra has always been hot-wired to what the late Flip Wilson called "The Church of the What's Happenin' Now," a temple where inside-out insights reverberate like so many silver dollars falling on a rock. The same sounds I hear whenever I recall **sound-advice**. The daily affirmations I commit to memory that adjust my attitude from one moment to another. Aphorisms like: "In the middle of difficulty, lies opportunity." Albert Einstein coined that one. Or how about, "Choose a job you love, and you will never have to work a day in your life." Confucius constructed that magnificent statement.

I repeat those pronouncements aloud. It's a devise I use repeatedly to keep me hot-wired to Flip's house of worship. Then, I can live and work on a direct plain with my friends —Yogi, Albert and Confucius. My private mentors who shoot straight from the hip and continually elevate my life. As a result, even when it's the bottom of the ninth with two outs and the count is three and two, I'm still ready to do battle. Yogi Berra once said, "Sometimes you win, sometimes you lose, and sometimes you get rained out; but you always get dressed for the ball game."

When I close my eyes I can still picture Mickey Mantle standing in the on-deck circle, or Yogi Berra throwing a runner out at second base. I can also visualize the best way to communicate my opinions and ideology by staying in the moment and practicing **the choice concept** and **sound-advice**. Recalling those early days when I attended baseball games with my Dad is a way to remember the past but remain in the moment. You might say that I feel the same way Garret Morris' character Chico Escuela from the original *Not Ready For Prime Time Players* felt, whenever he announced, "Baseball been berry berry good to me."

No one can make
you feel inferior
without your
consent...

Eleanor Roosevelt

Today, Tomorrow and Yesterday

As a teenager, I often felt as though I was in a giant canister overflowing with anxiety and jumbled emotions, convinced that the weight of the world had been placed on my shoulders. Of course, the real weight of the world occurs when you become a parent of a teenager; just ask my folks. Nevertheless, my insecurities were mine even if I was placing too much weight on my height, or height on my weight, not to mention my preoccupation with girls, hair, clothing, cars, girls, baseball, girls and ten thousand other seemingly important events. Like that wacky business between the United States and Russia. I believe they called it the Cuban Missile Crisis. Hell, what's all the fuss about a little nuclear annihilation among friends. Lets face it, that episode made everyone —not just teen-agers— a little jumpy.

In the summer of '62, when the Beatles were getting a foothold in the states and the Kennedys were in Camelot, I got a part-time job at the Bohack supermarket near Brighton Beach. I was also attending summer school for the second year in a row, because during the normal school year, I wasn't paying attention when those annoying trains came down the track. Those irritating trains that were generally carrying a ton of avocados, while heading toward Stubenville at the same rate of speed; one from St. Louis and the other from Miami. Suffice to say, if train number one stopped in Cleveland to make guacamole, I'd have a hell of a time calculating the Super Chiefs estimated time of arrival. Of course, I continued plodding along that difficult summer in 1962, until one afternoon a co-worker from the supermarket walked into the luncheonette where I was sipping a chocolate eggcream on a break, and unexpectedly reduced my shoulder-weight to a manageable mass.

Jim sat on the empty stool next to mine, smiled at the waitress behind the counter, and ordered eggs over-easy. He appeared to be about ten or twelve years my senior with a good sense of humor and a casual air. While Jim's eggs were sizzling on the grill, I sipped my soda and droned on about my teenage trepidations. Had Neal Sedaka written the melody to my words, I'm certain *Mikie's Teenage Lament* would have easily topped the charts.

Jim had the patience of a saint, smiling and nodding at the appropriate intervals until the waitress placed his eggs on the counter. After Jim popped a healthy dollop of ketchup on the eggs and cut them into tiny bite sized pieces, he announced, "Whenever I begin to worry about anything, I recall a simple proverb: 'Today is the tomorrow you worried about yesterday.'"

While Jim ate his breakfast, I reflected on his little aphorism for a moment, which I'm certain aided in his digestion. In the interim, I took a sip from my chocolate eggcream and Jim drank a little more coffee, and then he added, "Sometimes I recall that simple saying and it reminds me that worrying is a hollow emotion."

Until that time, no one had ever spoken to me that way, or if they had, I wasn't willing to listen. I recognized Jim's peaceful nature that day, and over the summer we became good friends. He had a beautiful family which he proudly displayed at the drop of a hat, frequently unfolding an accordion-like photo-holder from his weathered wallet.

Jim's harmony of heart and soul was always visible. He often chose his words with care and reflected for a moment before responding in kind. I believe Jim was pausing to give himself **sound-advice**, sound-bites not unlike the aphorism he'd mentioned during that first chance meeting we had at the luncheonette.

Jim's words represented the futility of worrying while cautioning against behaving like a victim. His advice was the kind of melody a fifteen year old needed to hum, rather than crooning the *Underdog Blues*. It would still take a few years before I stopped my complain-a-thon; however, it was a good start.

Throughout the summer Jim and I spoke about everything from the future of the country to the power of the Pontiac GTO. On my last day of work, Jim and I took our break at the tiny luncheonette across the street from the supermarket and I thanked him for his kind words. Words that would eventually become part of my current arsenal of **sound-advice**. I told Jim that I'd continue to remind myself that worrying was a useless emotion. We laughed and talked for a few minutes and then Jim said something I didn't quite understand. I wish I could say that I remained in the moment and told Jim that I hadn't grasped the meaning of his words, but I didn't. Yet, for some strange reason, I wrote the words down and years later I still had that small piece of paper, folded neatly in my wallet. The words on that tiny piece of paper proclaimed, "We only have now, keep it close." It was a generous message that seemed at first a bit cryptic, but over time its meaning became crystal clear.

It's all about spontaneity, choices and freedom. The words on that tiny piece of paper will always remain as a constant reminder to stay in the moment, which is precisely how my friend Jim lived his life. That tiny piece of paper also states that it's essential to step up to the plate whenever possible and make a difference in someone else's life, just as Jim had done for me. My friend knew that if he helped enough people get what they want, he'd get what he wanted, while at the same time he never offered unsolicited advice, knowing that if he did it might fall on deaf ears.

The weight of my philosophical friend's words remain firmly planted on my mind, never on my shoulders. He took the time to listen to a fifteen year old searching for answers and chose to offer his own brand of **sound-advice** as a gift. Jim was aware that I was self-critical because I was becoming self-conscious, that I was looking for solutions to questions that could only be found by looking within. He knew that the moment someone stopped looking outside themselves for answers, would they then be able to taste freedom.

About six months later, I ran into Jim and his wife at a restaurant in Sheepshead Bay. Jim's wife smiled when he couldn't resist showing me a recent photo of his two little girls. We spoke for a short while, but unfortunately that was the last time I ever saw my summer of '62 mentor. However, I often think about my friend Jim and wonder about the trials and tribulations he may have encountered over the years. My old friend's children probably have teenagers of their own, perhaps searching for a little guidance. If that scenario is taking place, I'm certain their grandfather is patiently listening to their hopes and fears before announcing: "Today is the tomorrow you worried about yesterday."

Our grand business is
not to see what lies
dimly at a distance,
but to do what lies
clearly at hand...

Thomas Carlyle

Dreams have as
much influence
as actions...

Mallarmé

Musical Interlude

A short while ago, I had a bizarre dream about the New York Philharmonic. Ordinarily, If someone said they'd dreamt about a prestigious orchestra, one might assume a restful nights slumber; however, in my dream, the symphony was playing Mozart's *The Marriage of Figaro* without taking beats or pauses. *Jarring* and *unpleasant* are the first two words that spring to mind.

In my fantasy, everything appeared slightly out of focus —soft and wavy— like a film style dream sequence viewed through a camera lens coated with Vaseline. Then all at once the entire event became crystal clear, except now the musicians were playing a Brahms lullaby with untuned instruments. My madcap slumber-fest appeared to be on an endless loop of haunting melodies, shattered vibrations and lullabies that would frighten a toddler napping at a pre-school. Not a moment too soon, the maestro began rapping his baton on the podium and the chaotic music abruptly ended. A moment later, the orchestra leader whirled around on his heels and faced the audience. His eyes were darting from side to side obviously searching for that certain someone. Instead of thinking please don't let it be me, I couldn't help but wonder where I'd seen his face before. Then it hit me. The orchestra leader was none other than famed character actor Joe Pesce. When I recognized Mr. Pesce, I immediately turned to see if the person sitting on my left thought it was surprising that he was at the helm of the New York Philharmonic. Dreams are often wonderful, and yet startling, because seated to my left was the Senator from New York and former first lady, Hillary Rodham Clinton. However, Senator Clinton didn't appear to be dismayed. "Jarring" may have turned into just plain weird about that time; so I decided to forgo the pleasure of finding out who was seated to my right.

Have you ever been in the middle of a dream and you can hear yourself saying, "This is a dream; it's time to wake up," but you can't quite snap out of it. Well, this fantasy had that element going for it. However, since the strange music had subsided, my star studded night vision didn't seem half bad. I'm not certain, but I believe at this point Mr. Pesce was smiling at me while extending an open hand. In any event, I returned his smile and reached into my pocket and began pulling out a king's ransom; gold coins, silver dollars and cold hard cash. In perfect dream-like fashion, the booty began floating in the air. Naturally, the audience was thrilled with my anti-gravity currency routine and began applauding, while back at the podium, Joe continued to smile at me with his hand extended. I couldn't tell you what Hillary was doing at the time. I may have been afraid to look. Anyhow, once again I reached into my pocket and this time I came out with a tuning fork. I handed the tuning fork to the academy award winning maestro and he quickly turned toward the musicians, tapped his baton to the podium and raised his arms to signal the beginning of the next piece; however, before the orchestra could play a single note, I was awakened by a kiss.

I wasn't upset when my wife interrupted my peculiar dream, because without my innocent wake-up call, I'm certain I wouldn't have recalled the illusion in the first place. Besides, in an attempt to make sense of the dream, I immediately wrote down as much of the fantasy as I could remember, although I believe Sigmund Freud may have found my unusual vision difficult to decipher. Nevertheless, later in the day all the pieces to my puzzling hallucination fit snugly into place.

In part, my vivid dream was the result of a discussion I'd had with a friend earlier that day. I'd driven to a music store in Berkeley that morning where I purchased a blues harmonica to use in my comedy act. Shortly after, I decided to grab a quick cup of coffee at The French Café, an outdoor café located in

Berkeley's "Gourmet Ghetto." I'm not certain if the residents of Berkeley had their tongues in or out of their cheeks when they dubbed that part of town, especially since most of the restaurants in the area wouldn't know gourmet food if they stepped in it. Moreover the least expensive home in the neighborhood would be a bargain at four hundred and eighty thousand dollars.

I'd been going there for quite a few years, because my friend Angel, a Mexican transplant with a great sense of humor, brews a mean cup of java. I marched up to the counter and ordered a café latté, and while Angel worked his magic with the espresso machine, I asked him —in my best high school Spanish— how his family was. When I turned around to locate an available table, I spied my friend Harvey waving at me from his customary perch in the corner of the café. I grabbed a seat at Harvey's table and before I could say Juan Valdez my quick cup of coffee had turned into a marathon —yes I'd love another refill— two hour extravaganza.

My conversation with Harvey, not unlike *My Dinner with André*, touched on a number of topics ranging from zero gravity to gun control. Harvey wasn't one to leave any stones unturned. At one point, Harvey mentioned that while I'd been on the road doing stand-up comedy, President Clinton had dined at the Chez Penise restaurant just across the street from the French Café.

Although, according to Harvey, after the prez dined at the upscale bistro, he and all the president's men made a bee-line to the nearest McDonalds. A stretch of the imagination indeed; however, the visual of our Supreme Commander ordering a happy meal and a vanilla shake, finally laid that business about the gourmet ghetto to rest.

Around my third refill Harvey and I began talking about the similarities between communication skills and music. I recall telling my friend that a conversation without beats and measures would be like listening to my favorite songs being sung by Donald Duck. I said that I love The Donald (that's Mr. Duck, not Mr. Trump), but that I don't care to hear either of them sing, "I left my heart in San Francisco." I prefer to leave that calling to Tony (The Bennett, not The Tiger). I was suggesting that just as the sound vibrations of tuned instruments, bring about pleasurable moments, **sound-advice** vibrations effect the beats and measures I use to communicate ideas.

"My *choice-voice* may compel me to sing a love song at the drop of a hat and create a wacky cartoon character a moment later," I announced. I told my old friend Harvey that for some folks it's all about *Miller Time*, but for me it's all about *carpe diem time*. I said that seizing the day is the cannon in my arsenal of choice weapons. Arms that line my pockets with all the cash I'll ever need.

My rhetoric struck a chord, because Harvey stood up and shouted, "Free drinks for everyone!" Of course, the café was empty at the time, except for a young woman seated at the next table, and she opted for a rain check. Seconds later I was demonstrating my theory by playing the blues on my harmonica and asking Angel —in Spanish— where the green elephants were hiding, a running gag I punctuated with the sound-effect of a trumpeting elephant. Come to think of it, maybe I should cut back on my caffeine.

While we were laughing, the young woman at the next table said, "Something has you in a really good mood."

I smiled and said that I hoped we hadn't disrupted her relaxing coffee break, but she insisted that our shenanigans had made her day. Kind words from a perfect stranger.

I thought about how she assumed I was in great spirits due to something external or perhaps artificial, when in fact it was something internal and genuine; that even if I was having a crummy day, I would never allow my emotions to dictate my attitude. Moreover, I consciously fend off the blues by playing the blues and sometimes by inquiring in Spanish where the large green five-toed mammals are hiding. **Sound-advice** reminds me to that. It also reminds me to celebrate the moment.

I thanked the young woman at the next table for her good nature, shook hands with

Harvey and Angel and made a hasty retreat —
always leave 'em laughin'.

Nearly every piece of my dream had fallen
into place. It was an illusion with a positive
message, one that reminds me to create glorious symphonies every day of my life —symphonies that never let me forget that the most
powerful component of a successful life, will
always be a good attitude. Jerry Gillies
asserts in his celebrated book *Moneylove*,
that without a good attitude, poverty consciousness may unknowingly become our
modus operandi; however, with the right attitude, we have the capacity to create all the
wealth we'll ever want. Mr. Gillies trusted his
inner voice and ran towards his dream. In
doing so, he wrote a best seller, which in turn
rewarded him with all the money he desired
and an exciting career as a motivational
speaker. Jerry taught me that when I actively
do the things I love to do, prosperity consciousness becomes second nature. He also
taught me to constantly reaffirm my own self-
worth, so I regularly proclaim that I deserve
the best that life has to offer. Jerry helped me
recognize that my success rests on my ability
to identify my strengths as well as my weaknesses, but never to dwell on either. However,
the most valuable lesson I learned from Jerry
Gillies was that if I didn't *believe* that I had the
power to create riches, how could I expect
anyone else to.

Now I practice my own **choice concept** ideology and **sound-advice** techniques, along with the creative ideas I've openly accepted in the past. The admixture has proven to be a blend of positive beliefs that have no room for excuses, explanations or intellectualizations. It's a powerful concoction, creating unlimited wealth and well-being, from one moment to the next. Ralph Waldo Emerson, the world renowned poet and writer, once said, "Man was born to be rich or inevitably to grow rich through the use of his faculties." His poignant statement reveals that obtaining wealth is simply a natural extension of my identity, that the key to material wealth and emotional fortune is clearly available to everyone provided we seize the day.

Just for the record, I wracked my brains in regard to the maestro in my bizarre dream about the New York Philharmonic, until I finally remembered that a few nights earlier I'd seen a George Carlin comedy special on HBO, and at the end of his monologue, George closed with a killer bit about God and Joe Pesce; henceforth, the beaming orchestra leader in the mist.

If you can imagine it,
you can achieve it.
If you can dream it,
you can become it...

William Arthur Ward

Whether you think that you can, or that you can't, you are usually right...

Henry Ford

Point of No Return

On an extended road warrior trip through the south, in search of a small comedy club in the great state of Alabama, I was about as lost as one human being could be without actually being in the wrong state. I'd swear on a stack of Bibles that I'd just driven past the same cow nine times; however, for a kid from Brooklyn who only viewed contented cows on the labels of evaporated milk cans, or the reoccurring stampede in a thousand Saturday afternoon westerns, Bossy could have been hoofing it from one meadow to the next and I wouldn't have a clue.

When I realized that I'd been given the wrong directions, bagging the club date and grabbing a hotel room began to sound like a pretty good idea. Visions of thick steaks and apple pies were dancing in my head, but then I recalled that annoying entertainer's credo, a ritual that likely had William Shakespeare performing the part of Hamlet at the Globe Theater because the actor who was supposed to play the part of the young prince came down with a case of the sniffles or the plague.

The same code of honor that coerces every performer into doing their little dog and pony act in the face of imminent disaster. Of course, I'm referring to "the show must go on." However, this show wasn't going anywhere without gasoline and directions, so I pulled into a musty gas station on a lonely dirt road, seemingly a million miles from nowhere.

At first glance, I thought the tiny gas station had gone out of business shortly after Henry Ford rolled the first Model T off the assembly line. However, upon closer inspection, I noticed a shopworn sign above the door that announced *Open for Business*. I backed the rental up to an antique gas pump with faded letters that read Texaco and topped off the tank. Then, I stepped inside a shanty that made Ted Kazinsky's shack look like the Taj Mahal. I thought a summer breeze could blow this hovel into next week, never mind a tropical storm. Seated behind a desk, that looked as if it had been dropped from the roof of the World Trade Center, was an elderly gentleman with a tuft of white hair on the top of his head and more lines on his face than Ben Franklin's portrait on the one hundred dollar bill. When the little bell on the door tinkled, he reached across the desk to turn down the volume on a tiny black and white television with pliers for an antenna, that was perched on a tray table next to the desk. Then he pulled out a pack of Camels and a pair of antique spectacles that had been sticking out of the top pocket of his

Ben Davis overalls. With his spectacles riding on the end of his nose, he began packing down the tobacco against the side of his hand and pulling off the strip of cellophane along the border of the smokes. I'd been trying to tell him where I'd driven from that morning and inquiring how I might get to my final destination, but I wasn't convinced he was even listening. Then with a broad smile he tilted his head, flipped open what appeared to be a pre-war Zippo lighter, and lit his cigarette. A moment later, after the obligatory *you're a long way off* had rolled off his tongue, he announced, "Son, yur between a rock an' a hard place. From where yur standin', it's as fur back to the beginnin' as it'd be if ya'll were to push on down the road." The old southern gentleman was telling me that I was at the point of no return, the same distance back as it was to my final objective, crossroads I'd encountered on a thousand highways across America for more years than I cared to recall.

I paid for the gas and a cup of coffee that Juan Valdez would have spent a year in a Colombian prison rather than drink. Then the good Samaritan began rummaging through his desk in search of "that durned map." A few minutes later, when I was just about to say: "Please sir just 'tell me' how to get there and I'll buy a case of Slim Jims and three mango air fresheners," my lethargic friend pulled out a road map that had more grease on it than Jerry Lewis' head. Slowly and methodically he explained where we were in relation to the rest of the western hemisphere and then finally he showed me how to reach my destination. In my entire life, I had never heard anyone speak as deliberately as this southern gentleman. I can't begin to describe how long it took him to tell me how to get back to the interstate. While he was talking, I kept thinking that I'd never missed a show before and that if he continued to give me directions, I might need a wake-up call. He meant well, but I wasn't taking any chances. So before he had the opportunity to pull out the graphs and charts, I thanked him and made a mad dash for the rental. Then, I rocketed down the road, and just one hour later, I arrived safe and sound, just a few minutes late.

As luck would have it, the opening act was a magician who was delighted to have more stage time. The club owner told me that the trickster had recently been to Las Vegas where he learned how to produce a flock of doves from God only knows where. Naturally, since I'd been on the road entertaining farm animals for the last three hours, he had the opportunity to perform his new illusion, which by the sound of the applause, went over quite well. Then, from the back of the comedy club, the owner gestured to the magician that I'd arrived. When he saw me standing next to the club owner, Svengali's expression was clearly one of relief. He was happy to do a disappearing act because his bird-in-the hand routine was —excuse the pun— his swan song. Before you could say

Shecky Green or Houdini, the magician brought me to the stage with a nice round of applause.

As soon as I hit the boards, I knew that if I had hand picked every individual in that audience, I couldn't have selected a better group of people. The room was packed and the spontaneous applause and serious guffaws were the best. I had them in the palm of my hand. When I was closing my act, it felt as if ten minutes had gone by, but in reality I'd been on stage for over an hour. The audience applauded until I had to climb back on the boards and do a forty minute encore. In a small town in the middle of nowhere, I'd clearly had one of the best sets I'd ever performed, but the night was still young. When I finally exited stage left, the club owner took me aside and said that I was the best comic he'd ever had in his club. Quite a nice compliment, considering a thousand funny men had rotated through the doors. He praised me further by saying that I was destined for bigger and better things, but that he hoped I might perform at his club again in the not too distant future. Then he asked the magician and I if we'd like the kitchen to broil up some steaks, and dish up a couple of pieces of pie for dessert. Our response to his question couldn't have been better if we'd rehearsed it. We looked at one another and then turned back to our host and simultaneously said, "If you insist." We were genuinely taken aback, considering the days of wine and roses had more or less ended for road warriors. Most of the clubs on the circuit were giving the entertainers a soft drink and a hardy handshake. I thought the owner's choice for the main course and dessert was interesting to say the least, considering that I'd visualized the menu several hours earlier.

Just when I didn't think the night could get any better, a blues band began setting up for a late night show. When the band was nearly ready to kick it off, one of the musicians came over to me and said that they'd heard me play the harmonica during my act and asked me if I'd like to sit in with them. I said that I'd be more than happy to jam on a couple of tunes and the night rocked on. That night I played the blues harp as if there really was magic in the air, Charlie Musclewhite would have been proud of me. They were talented musicians and their professionalism made me feel as though I'd been playing with them for years.

When the evening was winding down, I was talking with the singer in the band and I mentioned my trek through cow country and the little old man at the gas station. I told her about how I'd been at the point of no return and that I'd toyed with the idea of blowing off the club date. I said that ironically I'd even considered having a steak and some apple pie for dinner, and that although I'd been given lousy directions by the booking agent, I'd made the right choice to push on. She said she was glad I'd made that choice as well because the night had been special for everyone. I told her that I couldn't agree more, made my good-byes and drove on down the road.

Later that evening, I called my wife from my hotel room and I told her about the unique day I'd had. We laughed about the contented cows and the kind old gent with the spectacles and the greasy road map. Then my wife said, "Think about what you may have missed had you given up at the point of no return." I said that I couldn't agree more, then I gave her my love and told her to keep the home fires burning.

When I hung up, I began to think about how every success story had the same common denominator —the winners never turned back. When their business venture failed, they refused to accept defeat. If their little card shop burned down to the ground or a river went ballistic, they'd tighten their belts and rebuild. Repeatedly successful people visualize completed journeys, always mindful that perseverance isn't just an idyllic word but rather a right of passage. As I continued to lie on my motel bed, reflecting on my day, I recalled the imaginary snapshots I carry in my wallet; photographs of completed projects. Images I use to remind myself that life is an adventure and always a work in progress. Impressions and sound-advice that pay heed to whatever lies at hand, because it will always be just as far back to the beginning as it would be to push on. So why not choose to push on and on. Beyond the point of no return.

While we ponder
when to begin it
becomes too late
to do...

Quintillian

In nature there are
neither rewards nor
punishments —
there are
consequences...

Robert G. Ingersoll

Truth or Consequences

In the golden age of television, a popular game show called *Truth or Consequences* captured the attention of a million Americans. The game show's premise was straightforward. While one contestant was locked away in an isolation booth, the program's host, Bob Barker, would ask their better half, questions of a somewhat personal nature. If the questions were answered truthfully, the contestants received trips to Europe, cars and mounds of cash. However, if the participants were caught in a lie, they had to face embarrassing consequences in order to redeem themselves, and walk away with the booty. About that time, the host was heard to say, "Let's watch as the fun begins." If you've ever had the opportunity to witness a Japanese game show, our Asian friends seemingly lifted several of their ideas from *Truth or Consequences*, not that there's anything wrong with that; however, *Truth or Consequences* will forever remain the granddaddy of cruel and unusual game show punishment.

I can still recall one consequence that was particularly punishing. In truth, the writers likely reminisce about this one while swaying in their rocking chairs at the game show writers retirement home, somewhere in West Covina. They were obviously Machiavellian individuals, who took pleasure in placing a fat middle-aged balding man with glasses into a leather harness, and hoisting the poor bastard twenty-five feet in the air. To further humiliate the hapless fellow, the program's brain trust had him dangling precariously above the stage wearing nothing more than a diaper and a face clouded with fear. Did I mention that they attached a wire basket to this poor sap's shiny head? I'm surprised the producers didn't handcuff, shackle and blindfold this unlucky feed salesman from Nebraska. I'm certain, it just slipped their minds. Naturally, the studio audience was going wild. The scene was reminiscent of the classic story of *The Hunchback of Notre Dame*. In the timeless tale by Victor Hugo, the disfigured bell ringer, Quasimoto, is crowned King of the Grotesques by the poor people of Paris, and paraded through the streets. Our friend in the harness didn't have a hump, but that's where the similarity ended.

The next portion of our star-crossed friends ordeal, may have been where the golden-age television *fun* kicked into high gear. At that moment, the television camera panned over to our chubby friend's wife who was also wearing a face clouded with fear and an apron filled to the brim with farm fresh eggs. Her frightened expression was due to the balancing act she was performing on an enormous ladder just across from her husband. Hanging from the rafters in a diaper apparently wasn't embarrassing enough. The flying Wallenda's were about to enter *phase two* of their game show abuse. Of course, the object of the prank was for the marked man's bride to toss the eggs into the wire basket atop his head. If she was successful, a pot-o-'gold was theirs for the taking.

It's likely you can see the climax to this story coming straight down Broadway. Indeed, the besmirched yahoo ended up with more egg on his face than an arrogant politician at a concession speech. To add insult to injury, our diapered friend and his wife were eased off the stage with some lovely parting gifts from *The Speigel Catalog* and the ever present *Lee Press-on Nails.*

Someone once said that honesty isn't the best policy, it's the *only* policy. Whoever said that hit the proverbial nail on the head. The game show is long gone; however, telling the truth and accepting the repercussions for lying, remains constant.

If I dismiss the truth, I'm not likely to end up in a diaper with someone pitching eggs at my head. However, if I choose to disregard my *word* I still run the risk of removing scrambled eggs from every orifice on my face. Fortunately, **the choice concept** and **sound-advice**, reminds me that the truth is always easier to remember. It also recalls that every lie I've ever told is neatly filed away in my cerebral cortex, and since I don't enjoy the prospect of having lies hound my conscience throughout perpetuity, I prefer to tell it like it is. Within those perimeters the need to rationalize the truth and the temptation to fit someone's notion of who they think I should be, appears to be a waste of energy. In truth, I'd likely never measure up to someone else's expectations, nor would I care to.

I prefer to accent the truth, which in turn elevates every living thing around me. It's a style that gets easier all the time, free to concentrate on everything and nothing while sailing on wings of spontaneity —the very same wings young people sail upon whenever they feel safe. The wings of freedom I recall as a child —sitting on the kitchen floor, finger painting flawless masterpieces. Limitless images without boundaries. Now, once again, I've chosen to reason like a child who hasn't learned to accept failure, but more willingly chooses to embrace success. I've chosen to do so by accepting a simple system of positive reinforcement and repetition, and as a result my true potential is never given a glass of warm milk and sent to bed.

The celebrated motivational speaker Anthony Robbins believes that we all have a sleeping giant within eager to be awakened. I believe we also have a slumbering child within that begs to be called forth, a finger painter who understands success on an unconscious level. A child within, and without an ego. **Sound-advice** encourages that childlike naiveté. It reminds me to speak from my heart rather than my head. It's a choice-voice filled with imagination and strength. A voice that has always been there, and needs only a gentle reminder to reinforce the investment I call myself.

Robin Williams once said: "An error doesn't become a mistake until you refuse to correct it." Make no mistake, Robin stays close to his inner child, a child who reminds him to correct his errors from one moment to the next. He practices his own brand of **sound-advice**, which is why Robin is able to tell it like it is and frequently like it isn't. His brilliant style of comedy proves that things are not always what they appear to be; moreover, it confirms that if he was concerned with *what might be* and troubled by *what might have been*, he might overlook *what is*. Likewise, speculating about what might be hints at predicting the future, however the only real way to predict the future is by creating it. So, if I remind myself often enough to simply be myself, I'll not only create the future, but I may influence a few former finger painters and truth seekers to do the same. Besides, at the bare minimum, I'll never have to swing from the rafters wearing a diaper in front of a million Americans.

Nothing is
impossible to a
willing heart...

John Heywood

Get a few laughs
and do the best
you can...

Will Rogers

A Work in Progress

In college I experienced a lifetime of opportunity when I discovered courses in improvisation —improvising a scene by taking suggestions from the audience. Theater classes that were similar in form to the popular television program, *Who's Line is it Anyway.* It was a course of study that gave me a chance to create an original script from one moment to the next. I learned how to achieve an atmosphere of tranquillity one moment and unbridled enthusiasm the next. In one scene, I'd explore compassion, repulsion and ecstasy while moments later fear, lust and apathy.

Improvising proved a wondrous way to view the world. Although I discovered improvisational techniques in my mid twenties, I often refer to that time of my life as my formative years. The very moment I was bitten by the improv bug, I wanted to perform seven days a week. So, I looked outside my college courses and found Jim Cranna's class at The Old Spaghetti Factory in the North Beach section of San Francisco. It wasn't long after I began taking Jim's improv class, when he moved the Saturday affair to Fort Mason, in the Marina district. Nearly a quarter of a century later, Jim Cranna's classes are still going strong.

Jim Cranna is a consummate performer and one of the funniest men on the planet. His gifts range from hilarious dialects to biting commentary. While unbeknownst to most, Jim's dulcet tones and voice characterizations resound on radio ads from San Francisco to Mozambique.

Jim opens the Saturday session by telling his students that there are *no* rules in improvisation —except for *two rules*. You're not alone; it confuses everyone. Nevertheless, the two rules are: always act smarter than you are, and say 'Yes and.' In the world of improvisation, those rules are the main ingredients for every successful performance, and as I quickly discovered, they're not a bad road to travel in the real world as well.

Improvising taught me that the paragon for achieving success, both on stage and off, is a clear understanding of the concept of *support vs. denial*. Prior to my introduction to the world of improvisation, being supportive had been a hit-or-miss notion. However, the moment I climbed on stage, I soon learned that if a fellow actor began a scene by shouting, "The sky is falling!," and I proclaimed, "No it isn't!," my denial brought the scene to a screeching halt, while the entire audience visualized their cab ride home. I quickly learned that it didn't matter if Chicken Little was a mental defective from *One Flew Over The Cuckoo's Nest*, or my little chickadee turned out to be the big bad wolf disguised as Foghorn Leghorn. It was still key for the players to support one another —the audience demanded it. Granted, being supportive isn't a fresh revelation; however, considering most people are frequently exposed to all the denial they care to handle at the office, or at home, or in the bedroom, supporting your fellow actor proved essential. So, if the sky simply had to fall, perhaps dashing over to the supreme court where the law of gravity was being contested, might save the day, and the scene.

Improv classes not only demanded that I stretch the limits of my imagination on stage, they helped me recognize that being supportive was a powerful device off stage as well. However, supportive behavior wasn't an innate ability, it had to be practiced. The great statesman Bernard Baruch said, "In the last analysis, our only freedom is the freedom to discipline ourselves." So, not unlike a concert pianist rehearsing for an upcoming recital at the Royal Albert Hall, I practiced being supportive, until it became second nature. I recognized that by designing options from one moment to the next, I had the opportunity to provide the purest form of improvisation **—sound-advice**. It was a style that encouraged me to use creative diversions, little detours that regularly remind me that it's okay to be a work in progress, and that we can only do what we can, with the information we have.

Some years ago, the Coca-Cola Bottling Company announced the creative diversion; "Drink Coca-Cola; the Pause that Refreshes." Turning my head a silly millimeter without observing a billboard, or a bench at a bus stop that didn't have that axiom plastered all over it, was nearly impossible. It was a slogan that passed the lips of countless radio and television announcers, 'til the proverbial cows came home. Of course, after pausing and refreshing, I was bouncing off the walls from the caffeine and sugar crammed into every bottle, but coke still got my vote.

Now, I've chosen to give birth to my own creative diversion, a pause that stimulates better judgment by announcing: "You always have a choice!" It's a motto that dispenses compassion on a moment's notice, while reminding me to stay in the moment. It's the pause that observes that no one cares how much I know, unless they know how much I care.

Recently, my wife had the words *sound-advice*, engraved on a silver bracelet. She presented it to me on a Sunday afternoon, while I was reading the paper and said that it was a gift for no special reason. Now, whenever I step outside the moment, I look at my wrist and recall my partner's kindness and generosity. I recall her ability to create her own script from one moment to the next. It's a reminder to pause from time to time and take a deep breath and laugh at my own stubbornness, or my occasional reluctance to try something new. Her gift also reminds me that love is never conditional, and that success will always be my choice. Sometimes my silver bracelet even announces that it's Saturday afternoon —like now. And that if I don't hit the road, I might arrive late to Jim's Cranna's improv class.

Any idea seriously
entertained tends to
bring about the
realization of itself...

Joseph Chilton Pearce

There are only two ways
to live your life. One is
as though nothing is a
miracle. The other is as
though everything
is a miracle...

Albert Einstein

That's Entertainment

Whenever I feign a broad smile, I find it difficult to determine where the pretend smile ends and the real joy begins. Similarly, whenever someone laughs, I often feel compelled to laugh along with them, a reflex perhaps that's akin to witnessing someone yawn and responding in kind. While laughing satisfies a basic human need, it may also be demonstrating that life wasn't meant to be taken seriously. Don't misunderstand, I'm not advocating walking around with a silly grin on your face, especially since I've always been a little suspicious of anyone who smiles out of context, and who wouldn't. Likewise, whenever someone walks up to me and says, "Smile," I frequently have the urge to respond, "Bite me." Of course, I never say anything remotely comparable to a wisecrack of that magnitude, because if I did, the recipient of my ire may get the uncontrollable urge to perform the Mexican hat dance on my windpipe. Instead, I pause and say something funny like, "I wish I could smile, but I just found out my pet iguana needs contact lenses and my HMO doesn't cover eye care." Okay, so maybe "funny" was a bit of a stretch. How about whenever someone tells me to smile, I mutter something dumb. Either way, my friend stays confused and hopefully amused while I stay in the moment. The key element to my brief observation is that as long as I stay in the moment humor rules.

The first time I told my father I was going to do stand-up comedy he said, "You, a comedian!? Don't make me laugh." Dad's got a great sense of humor, and with a simple twist of fate Henny Youngman could have played second fiddle to my mom's wit and witticism as well. In a recent conversation with my mom, I was telling her about a friend who was obsessed with using puns, and without hesitation she declared, "Hanging is too good for him, he should be 'drawn and quoted.'" Maybe not mom's "A" material; however, not too shabby for the spur of the moment.

Our conversation evolved into the power of repetition, choices and **sound-advice**. A moment later, my mother was talking about the priceless literature that often guided her through her own life experience. "I frequently took comfort in the advice I gleaned from books by Eleanor Roosevelt, Thoreau and motivational speakers," she said. Then Marie paused for a second and said, "Although more often than not, I've been influenced by sound-bites and pearls of wisdom from late night television personalities." A statement that didn't surprise me considering my mom's been a fan of late night television since the early fifties when the late Steve Allen first hosted *The Tonight Show*.

"Steve Allen once said, 'If I can make people laugh, I can make people think,'" Mom announced.

I recalled the wisecracking monologist declaring, "If I can make just one person in the audience laugh, I'm in big trouble because everyone's gotta laugh or I'm out of a job."

Without losing a beat, my mother named her all time favorite, the former king of late night television, Johnny Carson. When it came to Johnny, my mom was practically a talk show groupie, which is understandable since she and my dad were contestants on a game show he hosted, shortly before he took over the reins of *The Tonight Show*. The program aired from 1957 to 1961 and resembled the Groucho Marx classic *You Bet Your Life*. Initially the program was dubbed, "Do you trust your wife?" Then, either they ran out of wives or decided to broaden their horizons, calling the show, *Who Do You Trust?*

As luck would have it, I had the good fortune to be with my parents when they got their fifteen minutes of fame. Earlier that day we'd taken the subway to Manhattan where the D train deposited the three of us at the Times Square Station. Then, my parents and I walked a few short blocks from Broadway and 42nd Street to Sardi's Restaurant around the corner from the American Broadcasting Company. I was feeling pretty important just walking around New York City and doing lunch at Sardi's, but that was just the beginning of what would prove to be a memorable day for our family.

My parents had been slated to appear on the program several times; however, whenever they got close to their moment in the sun, the previous contestants gobbled up precious air time, running a bit longer than the director had anticipated. Consequently, my folks kept getting bumped, which was a blessing in disguise considering every time they got bumped they got paid, and since my father worked in the evenings, there was never a conflict. In addition, the "bumped money" was practically the size of my father's weekly paycheck, so whenever the producers called Mike and Marie to come in and do the show, they were more than happy to oblige. Then, after mom and dad had been bumped three times in a row, something really wonderful happened. The producers showed their gratitude for my parent's patience by inviting them to have lunch with Johnny Carson at Sardi's Restaurant. My mother knew that it would be a thrill for me to tag along, so she asked the producers if it would be okay if I joined them, and they of course said yes.

I think it's safe to say that I was in shock during most of the actual lunch experience.

Lunching with television personalities at a trendy restaurant in Manhattan, shortly before my parents would step in front of the footlights of a popular game show, seemed positively surreal. I kept thinking that my friends will never believe me when I tell them why I'd missed school that day and that while they were having macaroni and cheese in the cafeteria, a waiter dressed in a tuxedo was bringing me a New York steak —if they could only see me now. However, I'm not certain if my friends would have recognized me even if they had seen me, considering I looked more like a deer caught in the headlights than a teenager at an eloquent Manhattan eatery. I still recall a few things about my brush with greatness; for example, whenever Mr. Carson said something it was often genuinely funny, while every time Ed McMann said anything, everyone appeared to be musing, "There's a joke in there somewhere, but we may have to organize a search party."

When we finished eating, Mr. Carson got to his feet first and said something to my parents while he was shaking their hands. Recently, my mom told me that Johnny wished them well, and said that he was glad they'd had a chance to talk. She also said that Johnny told them to have fun out there. Then Johnny turned on his heels and extended his hand to me and said, "It was nice to meet you Michael." I remember thinking how impressive it was that he had remembered my name.

I continued to shake Johnny's hand as I got up from my chair, and said that it was a pleasure to meet him. I was thirteen years old, but it still feels like yesterday.

A few minutes later, my parents and I filed out of Sardi's and walked around the corner to the ABC Studios. When we arrived at Studio A, a panicky fellow wearing a headset took us directly to the green room where a parade of people carrying clip-boards entered and exited with my parents' signature. In the midst of what appeared to be a controlled frenzy, a pretty young woman came in and began applying mom and dad's makeup. I recall smiling at my father while the makeup artist was putting powder on his nose; however, by then my dad had already gone beyond ordinary nervousness and didn't appear to see my tiny smile. I can't be certain, but I believe that just about that time my father was approaching a state of self-imposed terror. My mother seemed to be talking and laughing her jitters away, however it appeared that my father preferred to compose himself by slipping into full blown catatonia. I'm certain the makeup artist ran out of Max Factor's blush number nine considering my father's face made Casper the Friendly Ghost look like Michael Jordan.

Before I could wish my parents luck, the panicky individual wearing the headset arrived and quickly escorted me to the studio audience. Moments later, the applause sign above the stage was flashing and it was *show-time*. Ed McMann introduced Johnny Carson and we all applauded, then Ed introduced my parents and the applause sign lit up like a Christmas tree once again and everyone in the audience gave them a warm welcome. My mother hit the boards like a pro, she was on stage ready to entertain America. Dad, on the other hand, wore a frozen grin that made him look like a guy who'd had one too many face lifts. If it had been twenty years later, my father could have been a principle player in Mel Brooks' classic film *High Anxiety*.

Johnny asked my mother one question and she was off like a rocket, holding her own in front of the entire country. I thought that any second she might announce, "Yes, you are correct sir!" She was telling Johnny about dad's annual company convention and how she'd appreciate it if my father would take her along —just once. At one point she quipped, "I think it's about time he took me somewhere other than the A & P, don't you, Johnny?" The audience thought mom's one liner was terrif-ic. They were still laughing when she announced, "I'm at home with the kids, while he's sitting under a palm tree sipping one of those cocktails with the little umbrellas."

Laughter *and* applause. My mom was talk-ing so fast Johnny could barely get a word in edgewise. I was surrounded by three hundred strangers watching my mother and Johnny Carson perform a skit on national television and it felt great. I'm certain the producers were thrilled that Marie was engaging and animated. Her wacky story sounded like an episode from *I Love Lucy*.

Then, just when mom was getting warmed up, Johnny turned to my dad and said, "Mike, Marie seems to think you've been having the time of your life while she's at home changing diapers. How about it?"

Studio lights blazing, star-struck and in front of millions of Americans, the only sound my father could produce was a high pitched squeak. Without a glass of water dad was doomed. He sounded more like Pee Wee Herman on helium, than an insurance salesman from Brooklyn. While dad was making a gallant effort to respond to Johnny's question, Carson seized the moment by slowly turning toward the camera. At that moment, the soon to be knighted prince of late night television displayed what eventually would become his trademark expression —an ironic smile Johnny often used over the next thirty years at the helm of *The Tonight Show*. It was the same look of resignation Johnny used whenever a monkey climbed on his head and sat quietly eating a peanut, or when a guest answered his question with just one word. The same "look" Johnny's mentor Jack Benny had perfected years earlier, a *look* of pure genius. Then Johnny graciously handed my dad a cup of water, and while my father was taking a sip Johnny said, "I'm guessing right about now you're thinking 'I wish this drink had one of those little umbrellas in it.'" It was a brilliant call-back and the audience went wild. When the laughter and applause died down it was time to play, *Who Do You Trust?*

I still rib my father about his national television debut, but it's okay because I can outrun him. Besides, he and mom answered all of Johnny's questions correctly and won six hundred and fifty dollars, which was a nice chunk of change in 1961. It must have been a lot of money, because the following year my father took the entire family to the company convention in Miami Beach. In fact, there's an old family photo of my mother standing next to a palm tree by the pool at the Fountainbleu Hotel. Naturally, she's holding a drink with a tiny umbrella in it.

My mother created those wonderful memories when she wrote to the producers and asked to be a contestant on the program. She did so because she stayed in the moment and listened to her *choice-voice* and **sound-advice**. My mother continues to keep the moment close at hand with a mixture of humor, common sense and a large portion of love. Her countenance displays confidence, always extending and never pretending. It's an expression which reminds me of something the noted author and journalist Cyril Connolly once said, "We must select the illusion which appeals to our temperament and embrace it with passion, if we want to be happy." So every day I select a measure of comic relief from one moment to the next and choose the illusions that appeal to my temperament, and by doing so I'm happy as a clam. It's a simple system that I practice day in and day out. A simple procedure that continuously recalls Cyril's **sound-advice** and the advice of a thousand successful people like Johnny Carson and my mom and in my book *that's entertainment.*

He who laughs,
lasts ...

Repetition is
reality, and it is
the seriousness
of life...

Kierkegaard

Honest Exchange

I feel harassed whenever I ask someone how they are and they actually tell me, or when someone feels the need to unburden themselves by recounting that their kitty prefers *Little Friskies* and they're stuck with a ten pound bag of *Meow Mix*. At that juncture, I'm not only history, I'm hardly a distant memory. If I don't immediately turn into the invisible man or my head doesn't implode, I often feel compelled to deliver the straight skinny and let them know that my good nature has limitations. My commentary likely won't change their world; however, the very act of honest exchange reinforces the moment and empowers my world.

What's worse than smalltalk on a grand scale? If there's a punch line to that joke, I haven't been able to find it. The only tag line I can come up with is *nothing, zip, zilch, zero*. I invite people to talk with me, "really talk with me." I deserve emotions, insights and dreams —nothing less. I'm not certain; however, I believe the word smalltalk may come from the Latin *To Bore* as in "Your twaddle is 'boring' a hole in my head." My modus operandi strives to be candid with no substitutions. If I'm not being completely honest, my relationships are only illusions at best. I prefer to share my weaknesses as well as my strengths, and if I begin to employ the "I can top that" notion, or the always popular "there isn't anything you can tell me that I don't already know" syndrome, my guardian angel sends up a flare that warns me that I'm about to engage in a pompous attitude that only serves to create distance rather than dialogue.

When dialogue comes in the form of honest exchange, **sound-advice** easily acknowledges the human condition, quickly filling the gap between safety and spontaneity. Honest exchange is a fresh side of life that challenges rehearsed chatter and preconceived rationale. It compels me to make listening my prime function. I've heard it said that God gave us two ears and one mouth so we can listen twice as often as we speak. When I really listen, I'm never preoccupied with interjecting pearls of wisdom. If I have an original idea, I'll speak-up, if I don't, I won't. When I'm *really listening*, I've chosen to participate, eager to connect rather than pretending to connect. At that moment, I'm sharing my strengths as well as imperfections. Anything less and I may as well be walking along a crowded street having a conversation with myself. "Anything less" constitutes not being present, and if I'm not present, my opinions are hollow notions coming from someone who just gabs to hear the sound of their own voice.

History books are crammed with presidents who had to account for hundreds of people, yet somehow they were still able to call their trash collectors by their first names. They were able to do so because they were great listeners. Without question, an intelligent individual will always give you his or her undivided attention; that's why bright people tend to respond to questions a tad slower and attach more conditions to their answers, revealing that they may not be certain more often than not. Keen individuals are apprised of their own limitations and aware of the effort it takes to consider life's complexities. They simply want the biggest bang for their buck —the ultimate response. Moreover, great listeners are quick to recognize what Nietzche called *The Tarantulas*. Individuals who can't improve their own place in the world, so they devote their energies to tearing down others. Albert Einstein attested to that notion as well when he proclaimed: "Great spirits have always encountered violent opposition from mediocre minds."

Einstein's classic comment, like his timeless theory of relativity, is pure gold. The thought of a mediocre mind impeding the good doctor's ultimate goal is laughable, yet average individuals attempted to disprove his genius, only to witness an immovable force determined to capture time in a bottle. I regularly recall the renowned physicist's time-honored remark, especially when I'm confronted with second-rate sarcasm and narrow minded people. As quickly as I can recall Albert's **sound-advice**, my own great spirit emerges confident and controlled. In truth, in that cool moment, it becomes easy to recognize the tarantulas and the mediocre minds. In that cool moment, I'm once again reminded of my game plan because, unfortunately, the *desire* to overcome mediocrity is never enough to achieve greatness. But with a game plan, a mountain of accomplishments are there for the asking.

Dennis Waitley, the celebrated motivational speaker, said, "Fail to plan, plan to fail." His simple statement brings it all home. Without a plan or a procedure to stay on target and realize our dreams, someone else may walk away with them. In a related story, I recently read about a medical doctor who became a healer at the age of forty-one. The good doctor revealed that he'd received his Bachelor of Science degree years earlier, but instead of listening to **sound-advice**, he dismissed his dream and became a certified public accountant. "I just let it happen," he said. "For years I regretted not listening to my inner voice." The physician went on to say that he believed that the secret to success is to choose a plan and then take action. "At last I chose to listen to the small voice that challenged every obstacle in my path," he said. The voice that kept repeating that it's never too late to run toward your dreams." The physician said that now, when he awakes in the morning, he can hardly wait to get to work. He said, "If I hadn't burned the midnight oil for four years, I'd still be four years older; the only difference is I'd still be a CPA."

The great playwright Noel Coward once said, "Work is more fun than fun." His work became his passion, a continuous labor of love. Great thinkers like Noel Coward, and courageous individuals like the good doctor, provide me with the strength to surpass ordinary life and attend to *extraordinary* life. In part, I'm able to reach my own goals because I've chosen to listen to successful people and emulate their values and work ethics. Not unlike the number-crunching physician, I frequently challenge every obstacle in my path, mindful never to build barricades of my own. I'm also aware that a treasure is never revealed unless the treasure hunter physically takes the action necessary to uncover the booty.

The **choice concept** and **sound-advice** are treasures I uncover from one moment to the next. It's an alliance of knowledge and common sense, a union that helps me gain insight into ecstasy and a technique that replaces careless judgments with careful convictions. Now I have options as well as opinions and a voice on an endless loop that announces, "Soar with the eagles, not with gobblers; turkeys, not unlike misery, love company."

Speak kindly today;
when tomorrow
comes you will be
in practice...

Anonymous

If the only tool you
have is a hammer,
you tend to see
every problem as
a nail...

Abraham Maslov

Sammy, Delilah and George Bailey's Wonderful Life

Picture the legendary Iron Sam and his sweetheart Delilah sipping a quaint Merlot by the fire, a creamy Norwegian Brie rests in the center of the mantle. In the middle of the bedroom chamber, a box of Fat Free Triskets teeters on the edge of a Henredon coffee table. Delilah's sitting on a bear skin rug, dressed in a silken-toga-teddy and is casually flipping through the pages of Gentleman's Quarterly, while Sam lounges on a vibrating E-Z Boy with the television clicker, randomly channel surfing. Suddenly, Delilah announces that Samson's hairstyle —piled higher than the pyramids— might be a touch out of style. It seems Delilah caught a glimpse of Keanu Reeves on the cover of GQ, and now she's convinced that Sam's pompadour looks like something from the Sumarian Age.

The following day, after a few hours of gentle but firm coaxing from the lovely Dee,

our man of steal decides to drop by his coif-
fure for a little pruning. "I'd like the 'Keanu
Cut,' Mr. Larry," Sam announces upon his
arrival at Larry's Clip Joint, a quaint tonsori-
um located between two Starbucks, adjacent
to the Coliseum. Mr. Larry, affectionately
known as *porcupine head*, and a man of few
words, smiles knowingly and then does whatever comes naturally.

Later that day when Sam returns home,
Delilah informs Charlie Atlas that he looks
more like Moe from The Three Stooges than
Keanu Reeves. Although our hero is a little
wounded, he's still determined to get the
Keanu cut, to please his sexy Delilah. Sammy
immediately returns to Ye Old Barber Shop,
feeling a little punier than he did earlier that
day, but thinks nothing of it. When Sam walks
in, he announces that the hair cut he'd
received wasn't quite the look he had in mind.
So, he asks porcupine head to give it another
shot. Smiling a bit out of context, Larry nods
and drags out the heavy equipment, and for
the next forty-five minutes he gets uncom-
monly creative with Sammy's head. When all
is said and done, Sam no longer resembles
Moe from the famed threesome, however now
he bears an uncanny likeness to Curly and
Jesse Ventura. To add insult to injury, when
Delilah catches a glimpse of Sam's hairdo, she
exits faster than Sammy's strength. In fact,
Sam is so weak that not only is pumping iron
hopeless, pumping gasoline is nearly impossi-

ble. It appears that Iron Sam's strength was removed one snippet at a time. Hold on to your hair-weave, here comes the moral to my wacky allegory.

Like the gradual loss of Samson's strength, when I fail to keep the moment close at hand, I not only run the risk of a bad hair day, I run the risk of a bad hair *life*. In fact, my chances of ending up with stringy ethics and unmanageable morals remain a strong possibility. However, since I've designed my system of total recall, I'm able to re-shape my decision making skills and firm-up my ideology on a moment's notice. Consequently, I've come to the conclusion that if swimming builds the muscles of my body, exercising *The Choice Concept* and **sound-advice** empowers my soul. My simple formula creates flawless hair days, and that's quite an adventure for yours truly, considering I'm bald —make that *hair-challenged*. Just for the record, I'm not *losing* my hair. I know exactly where it is, it's around the drain in the shower.

Henry David Thoreau, the most significant author and naturalist of the twentieth century, said: "If you build castles in the air, your work need not be lost; that is where they should be. Now put the foundations under them." Humor is the foundation for all my castles. It's a practiced attitude that responds to the right choice at the right time.

The Choice Concept and **sound-advice** are akin to the song *The Rose*, which affirms, "It's the heart afraid of dancing that never learns to live." I offer another line from a song of laughter that maintains, "It's the heart within the moment that learns to live forever."

Singing the praises of **sound-advice** taught me that my life can be whatever I decide it should be; however, in order to make my dreams come true, the first thing I had to do was to wake up. Now I'm wide eyed and bushy tailed and I regularly validate the honest reflections that adjust my attitude one snippet at a time. In addition, I steadfastly honor the life I've been given every moment of every day.

The champion storyteller Frank Capra illustrated *honoring one's life* better than anyone ever has in his classic film *It's a Wonderful Life*. In the director's brilliant adaptation of a story written by Philip Van Doren Stern and Frances Goodrich, the main character, George Bailey, faces imminent financial ruin at the hands of his nemesis. Tormented and suicidal, his life hangs by a thread, when our hero finds himself in the hands of a cherubic savior in pursuit of wings. In the ensuing film, George is locked in a nightmarish journey while his messenger of hope demonstrates how a seemingly ordinary life can touch the lives of countless others. It's an inspirational tale proving that each chapter of our lives is filled with richness, but that ultimately it's the journey across the pages that shapes who we are.

The private messenger of hope I call **sound-advice** reminds me every day that I've been given a gift, and the techniques I continually practice keep me in sync with nature. Athletes call it *the zone*, that place where the overwhelming desire to achieve success hurls baseballs across stadiums and propels footballs over goal posts. My private messenger reminds me that without a positive attitude and a continuous convoy of humor, I'm likely to watch the foundation of my castle turn to dust one snippet at a time. I practice the formula freely, using random acts of kindness and recalling words of wisdom from a plethora of unique individuals, and that allows me to stay in the moment with nary a "hair" out of place.

Everything I did in
my life that was
worthwhile I
caught hell for...

Earl Warren

If you find your inner
conversation running
along negative lines,
you have the power
to change the
subject, to think
along different
lines...

Martha Smock

Smokin'

Eddie and Kenny climbed inside a billboard on a vacant lot near Nostrand Avenue, and I followed. My cousins were the older brothers I never had, so I followed them everywhere —whether they liked it or not. One side of our secret hiding place declared: "Smoke Kent's with the Micronite Filter," while the opposite side revealed a carton of *Camels* a tad smaller than an aircraft carrier. The Kent side of the billboard pictured a doctor and a nurse enjoying a relaxing smoke in the corridor of a hospital. I imagine Flo Nightingale and Doc Holiday were sharing a quiet moment after performing a triple bypass, or perhaps they were pausing to catch their breath after completing their rounds on the emphysema ward. The Camel ad displayed a rugged male model sporting a hard hat and a tool belt standing next to a construction site. The caption above his head proclaimed, "I'd walk a mile for a Camel." A few years later I believe he became the construction worker with the Village People and helped popularize the catchy tune *Y.M.C.A.*

The powerful tobacco lobby wasn't about to leave any stones unturned. They had commuters smoking their brains out en route to Manhattan or heading toward the Cyclone in Coney Island. Coincidentally, my cousins and I were sandwiched between the gargantuan ads with the express purpose of smoking cigarettes with or without micronite filters.

I'm not certain which relative handed me my first smoke or who extended the Zippo to fire it up; however, I'm convinced that the crud on the bottom of my Keds couldn't have tasted any worse. Naturally, every time I sputtered and coughed, my cousins roared with laughter. They'd obviously been at this smoking business for some time considering they knew how to take a deep drag, a swallow from a Coke, and exhale all at the same time. It was a piece of business the detectives on *Naked City* demonstrated whenever they drank coffee in the squad room, or when they were unveiling the murder victim of the week down in the morgue. In truth, all the crime fighters on television in the 1950s had cigarettes dangling from their lips and smoke billowing about their faces. However, the police and the private eyes weren't the only ones lighting up on television. Everyone from baseball players to actors wearing scuba gear called for Philip Morris or the toasted flavor of a Lucky Strike. While exposing the communist witch hunt being conducted by the infamous Senator Joseph McCarthy and his merry men, noted broadcast journalist Edward R. Murrow would have appeared uncharacteristic without a cigarette in his hand. And, the now defunct Joe Camel couldn't hold a candle to the likes of Lucille Ball and Desi Arnez, unless of course Lucy and Cuban Pete were borrowing his candle to light the Pall Mall cigarettes they touted on *I Love Lucy*.

My cousins and I were in our asphalt-jungle tree house towering above well-worn sidewalks discussing important issues like smoke-ring blowing, the French inhale and the correct way to hold a cigarette or light one. They were important issues because we had to be certain we were displaying the optimum air of "cool." We wanted to hold a smoke the same way Bogart and Mitchum held their smokes, especially when they did a scene with Lauren Bacall or Veronica Lake. We wanted to fire up a cigarette the same way Kirk Douglas fired up a smoke just before he smacked some wiseguy across a room, or tossed a hoodlum through a plate glass window. My cousins and I figured if we emulated those larger than life characters, we'd be tough and cool too, or at least as tough and cool as three kids perched inside a billboard on a vacant lot in Brooklyn can be.

Of course I couldn't admit to my cousins that I thought a cigarette tasted like volcanic ash, and that if my father got wind of the twelve year old Marlboro Man living under his roof, my tonsils might come out through my nostrils long before filtered cigarette smoke. So with smoke blasting through my nose, I growled, coughed and pawed at the scaffold I'd been doing a balancing-act on inside a rusty billboard thirty feet above Nostrand Avenue. I'm sure I looked more like a bull chasing a rodeo clown on a cold day in Montana, than a snot nosed kid puffing on a cigarette in a billboard in Brooklyn.

When the deed was done, my cousin Kenny placed the pack of smokes in his sock, reached into his pocket, and doled out three Chicklets, then we climbed down from our den of iniquity and hit the ground running. Bounding over rusting bicycle frames and broken bottles, we raced across the vacant lot and around the corner to my house on East 29th Street. Moments later, we sprang up the front steps and rushed toward the kitchen where my mother and sister had been preparing our lunch. However, before we could put a spoonful of Bosco in a glass of milk, my cohorts and I listened quietly to a bizarre conversation my mother was having with my sister.

Mom was opening jars of peanut butter and grape jelly and openly talking about an article she'd read that morning in the Daily News. Incredibly, the article in the newspaper had been about cigarette smoking and the diseases connected with the damaging habit. To hear my mother summarize the article one would think she was describing a scene from

Dante's Inferno; painting her own frightening portrait of black lungs, hospital wards filled with pain and misery and last, but not least, halitosis.

Like three puppies listening to Wayne Newton sing Dankashein, our pointed heads were tilted to the side staring at one another in amazement. How could my mother casually discuss the downside of smoking just after I'd tried the vile weed for the first time? Was it just an extraordinary coincidence or was she simply toying with us? Had she detected smoker's breath when we kissed her upon our arrival? Impossible we were all chewing Chicklets. Smoke signals rising above the billboard? Naturally our tiny smoke-filled brains couldn't comprehend that my mother's extrasensory perception was due to the aroma emanating from our clothing. The only thing my mother said when she placed the food on the table was, "Don't talk with your mouths full." Then she promptly disappeared. We of course remained clueless, shrugged the entire incident off and continued our quest to imitate the Three Stooges.

Years later my mother recalled her one act play in the summer of '59. She said that the moment we walked through the door she noticed that our clothing had a distinct odor. "Not an odor associated solely with smokers," she said, "but rather with people who smoked while harvesting the back forty on an R.J. Reynold's tobacco plantation." My mother said that she was hoping her veiled description of diseases and bad breath might deter us from any further experimentation.

In retrospect, my mother's child psychology worked wonders on me. Cigarettes were one bad habit I never acquired. My cousins, on the other hand, didn't fare as well. Not long after we blew smoke-rings in our secret hideout above Nostrand Avenue, Eddie and Kenny were hopelessly addicted. Jokingly, Eddie used to say that he preferred a Camel because the micronite filter in a Kent blocked out too much tar. Kenny told me that he was trying the nicotine patch. Then, he said that he was up to three patches a day. I, of course, told them that I preferred to smoke a Salmon, although I found them a little difficult to keep lit.

After a thirty year, two-pack-a-day habit, my billboard smokin' buddies *chose* to call it quits. They sighted several discussions we'd had in the past about the **choice concept** and **sound-advice** as a major factor in their decision making process. I felt great when I heard them say that **sound-advice** had contributed to ending their addiction to cigarettes, especially since we'd never spoken about their addiction, but rather about visualization, choices and taking control of our lives.

My cousins chose life rather than allowing life to choose them. They said that quitting was the most difficult thing they'd ever done.

My cousin Kenny said, "The key was in the reminders I continually used that prompted me to replace bad habits with good ones. When I finally grasped the true concept of choice," he said, "I was half way there."

Shortly after Kenny quit, cousin Eddie followed suit. When I spoke to Eddie on the phone, he said, "I finally *believed* that I had the power to stop smoking forever. I visualized a smoke-free life and it looked a hell of a lot better than being a slave to cigarettes."

I understood Eddie's new found awareness because the concept of visualization was a devise I'd been using for years.

Some time ago I learned that research had proven that the mind can not distinguish between reality and what is visualized as reality; however, unless we visualize what we want continuously, our mind may find the concept difficult to grasp. Today, **sound-advice** reminds me to visualize wealth in precise numbers and my conscious mind fashions ways to make those numbers reality. I visualize good health as well and my conscious mind keeps me fit. I visualize the things I know I deserve and my mind invents ways to create the character I need to achieve my goals and the integrity to acquire all that glitters. Sir Winston Churchill once said that the future is in our hands and that our lives are what we choose to make them. I choose to build a monument to better judgment, measured moments that grant me the calm I need to attain all the success I desire. While book-shelves may be lined with publications on *how to,* now I simply *choose to.*

The renowned English novelist, William Makepeace Thackeray, expressed a bit of wis-dom I use daily in my **sound-advice** arsenal. He said, "There are many sham diamonds in this life which pass for real, and vice versa, many real diamonds which go unvalued." When I practice the concepts of choice, sham diamonds are revealed to me at once, allow-ing precious stones to take center stage. It's a sound philosophy that unmasks zircons and lays open strands of cultured pearls from one moment to the next; but don't just take my word for it, ask my cousins.

The truth is more
important than
the facts...

Frank Lloyd Wright

It is your work
in life that is
the ultimate
seduction...

Pablo Picasso

Magic Dust

In the early eighties, I lived in a city referred to by some as "The Center of Enlightenment," while others a tad wiser simply called it *Berserkley*. In a moment of weakness I had the strange misfortune to seek employment in the automobile industry, a career I pretended to be suited for while in my heart, entertaining America was where I needed to be, *or not to be*. Anyhow, I hadn't accepted the moment nor was I paying attention to the sound of my own voice, so I awoke one morning and found myself selling Japanese automobiles. Don't get me wrong, for some people, selling automobiles may be a noble profession, but for me a plethora of alternatives loomed in the distance.

My tenure as a car salesman lasted three short months, or in the vernacular of the car business, I was blown out in 90 days, an event which came as quite a surprise considering I was prompt, courteous and sold more automobiles than several of my peers. Nevertheless, I was sitting behind my fat desk in my little cubicle, completely unaware that the ax was about to fall on my Armani shirt and color coordinated Evan-Picone tie. Suddenly, I felt a strange chill. Come to think of it, a strange chill would have to be the understatement of the decade. I felt more like Father Dimitrios standing next to Linda Blair's bed in *The Exorcist*. Not exactly a chill that could get your head spinning, but it was close enough for Jazz.

When I finally got the courage to look up from my desk, I realized that the icy conditions were emanating from the sales manager's office. On closer inspection, my boss appeared to be leering at me from inside his little glass house the same little glass house where for the past ninety days I'd been bringing him "the deals." Of course, before I brought him the deals, I was required to give each client the customary song and dance routine: "Well sir, I'm not sure if your offer will fly, but let me take it into my manager and see what he thinks." Then I'd take two steps in the direction of the manager's glass portal, turn back momentarily, and announce, "Keep smilin'. I'm gonna make you an owner." It's enough to make anyone lose their lunch, however, now it appeared that my manager was about to make me an offer I couldn't refuse. Because the next thing I heard, was the sound of his door snapping shut and when I looked up, he was half way across the showroom floor —heading in my direction. However, before he could reach my desk, another salesman stopped him in mid-stride. Although, while they were talking, his eyes were still eerily transfixed on me and my tie.

While he was standing there discussing a business transaction with my cohort, and staring at me intently, I couldn't help but recall the first time I laid eyes on this cretin. I remembered how much he reminded me of Washington Irving's character Ichabod Crane. The legendary young man from tale of the headless horseman. Although, shortly thereafter, I determined that he more closely resembled the headless horseman's chestnut mare, tall and thin with a long face and a pony tail —clearly a horse's ass. However, his features were a small part of what one might consider, a bounty of hinky quirks. Whenever he spoke, he tilted his head to the left at a forty-five degree angle, the identical head-tilting action a certain talking horse displayed whenever he spoke. However, his head-tilting maneuver was the least of his peculiarities, because while he was tilting and talking, his lip would involuntarily raise-up on the left side of his mouth, ala Elvis Presley. To add insult to injury, he squinted as though he needed glasses. Oddly enough, he was already wearing glasses. Consequently, if one were to look up the phrase "beady eyes" in the dictionary, I'm certain this fellow's photograph would be glaring back at you. The sad part about this bizarre fellow, was that he put more snow up his nose than the yearly ground cover at Heavenly Valley, which I'm certain accounted for his irrational mood swings and overall vile disposition.

When he finally arrived at my desk, he stood there looking down at me for a second. Then he quickly leaned over and placed his clenched fists on the legal pad I'd been doodling on, just before I'd noticed a drop in the temperature. His long horse face was roughly two inches from the tip of my nose. I thought for a second that he was going to kiss me. Of course I knew that was impossible, especially since his lip was arched so high it was practically above his pointed snout. In the same creepy monotone he used whenever I brought him an offer from a prospective buyer, he quietly hissed, "We need to talk." However, before I could say word one, he turned on his heels and walked back to his office. I did the last mile walking slowly behind him, zigzagging around the shiny new automobiles until we arrived at ground zero.

"Kindly close the door behind you," were the last words I heard *Mr. Smarmy* —a fitting name my friend David had given him— say. I really couldn't tell you what he said after the office door snapped shut. I only know that whatever he was trying to say sounded more like psycho-babble than anything I'd ever heard before or since. When I walked out of his office, I wasn't sure if I was supposed to get donuts for the parts department or report to the unemployment office. Although, I had a strong feeling I was out of a job when he erased my name from the chalkboard roster behind his desk. Especially since he began erasing my name just after he said, "Kindly close the door." He even had the gall to utter the same phrase, when I was on my way out. Although, by then the request line was closed so I ignored him and pushed the door open a little further. I zigzagged around the cars again, cleaned out my little cubicle and told my co-workers that I was fairly certain I wouldn't be receiving a gold watch. They nodded in agreement and off I rode into the sunset.

The following day, my friend David phoned to tell me that I had a good case against the company for wrongful termination. He said that Mr. Smarmy began the morning sales meeting by saying, "In case anyone is curious I fired 'Joke-Boy.' He was having too much fun." I told David that I took his critique as a compliment. I always knew I could be a mediocre car salesman, but that if I ran toward my dream, I could be a great Joke-Boy.

My ultra-short car sales career was worth its weight in gold. I met several genuine human beings that became life-long friends. I'm certain that may sound a tad suspect, considering the general consensus seems to be that car salesmen are well below leeches on the evolutionary scale, an opinion held by the majority of people around the globe. A well founded opinion, I might ad, stemming from the nightmarish experience commonly called *buying a new car* and then paying nine hundred dollars for floor mats. Or perhaps after signing on the dotted line, finding the phrases *payments throughout eternity* and *first born male child* cleverly concealed in the fine print.

Nevertheless, before I was sacked, I met a few kind souls and managed to learn a thing or two about the psychology of selling. For example, whenever a customer was talking to me, I looked directly at their lips, and if the customer's lips were moving, they were generally lying. Of course they did so because they were afraid I might find out where they'd hidden their money. Or perhaps they were a tad paranoid, resulting from years of Pavlovian bells and whistles, artfully dangled in front of their faces by smooth talking sales associates and finance managers. Those slippery men and women who pick over weary bones with extended warranties and inflated protection plans, until the thoroughly exhausted buyer is left with barely enough money to pull up to the drive-up window at McDonald's in his or her new automobile and order a Happy Meal.

The sales people fault the customers for their behavior, alleging the client repeatedly forces their hand; however, I witnessed the game from both sides of the desk and recall lies flying from side to side. Untruths which accounted for the sprinkling of "be-back dust," imaginary powder I'd reach into my pocket and scatter above my customers' heads as they sauntered out the front door. I performed that little maneuver every time a customer, who didn't bare the slightest resemblance to Arnold Schwarzzenagger, announced "I'll be back."

In the car business, one needs the tenacity of *The Terminator* and the skin of an Alligator; however, for me, getting the job and getting the boot were blessings in disguise. "You weren't fired, you were liberated," my friend David once said. He added that by getting sacked I had achieved success faster than anyone he'd ever met. David recognized that in part my short-lived car sales career had created a tiny seedling which ultimately blossomed into the **choice concept** and **sound-advice**. The formula that provides individuals with successful futures in their chosen profession, a recipe which affirms a procedure I didn't fully understand at the time, but would eventually come to cherish.

Novelist Ralph Ellison once said, "Freedom ain't nothing but knowing how to say what's up in your head." I say what's up in my head with enthusiasm, and while I'm at it, I throw in a measure of love. I do so by recalling a blueprint that demands elevated decisions, choices that shape my life from one moment to the next. The choice concept is a simple system of repetition and rediscovery, all day every day. Moreover, it creates the confidence everyone needs to move toward a clear understanding of what we do best. When that occurs, every day is filled with spontaneity and freedom.

In the final analysis, I know that my self-worth had nothing to do with my boss's opinion of me. That in order to achieve success, I had to recognize the void inside, and outside myself, and figure out how to fill it. Simply put, life runs a hell of a lot smoother when we accept who we are and who we're capable of becoming, cognizant that choices never spring from a sorcerer's black bag filled with magic dust, but rather by attending to that small voice within.

Whatever people
think of me is
none of my
business...

Mary Tyler Moore

Remember the story of the Spanish prisoner. For many years he was confined in a dungeon...One day it occurred to him to push the door of his cell. It was open; and it had never been locked...

Winston Churchill

A World of Wonder

When the summer heat blistered the tar atop the streets of Brooklyn and the setting sun produced little relief, my parents would take my sister and I to a place where cool breezes from the ocean swept across our tiny faces and magic filled the air. The popular Island of Coney was once a beautiful summer resort separated from the mainland by a small channel of water. In the heat of the day, sun-baked New Yorkers cooled their heels in the Atlantic while faint screams of terror emanated from monster roller coasters with commanding names like *Cyclone* and *Thunderbolt*; heart-thumping speed-wagons producing G forces that astronauts routinely face when traveling in space shuttles rocketing to the moon.

In the distance, the towering lights from the Wonder Wheel created an imposing backdrop as our little family walked along the midway listening to carnival barkers shout: "Three throws for a quarter!" Taking the challenge, my father would often strike the milk bottles center stage; however, the bottles were likely made from a mixture of white lead and titanium and couldn't be knocked over with the family car. Of course my sister and I would happily settle for a pair of Groucho glasses or a large toothy comb.

If I close my eyes I can still hear the sound of calliope music and picture my dad with his arm around the cardigan that rested on my mother's shoulders while my sister and I chased one another along the wooden boards above the sand. We'd often tarry along the boardwalk and listen to honky tonk piano players or singing cowboys at the open air cafes. The same way my grandparents had paused with their children, a generation earlier. My dad recalls Will Rogers performing rope tricks in front of Luna Park, and stopping by Nathan's to support his father's friend. A gravely voiced piano player with a big nose from the Bowery, named Jimmy Durante.

On those balmy summer nights, when the dinner bell rang, my family and I would sit on wooden benches facing the drumming surf, sipping orange drinks and munching hot dogs from Nathan's Famous. If the gods were in a generous mood and it happened to be a Tuesday night, the muted sky above the Atlantic might explode in a splash of color. Multicolored rockets launched from barges soared above the sea, while moments later, when the mist above the ocean was once again dark and the last bite from a dog gone, two sleepy children were nestled in the back seat of a '56 Chevy heading home. On a warm summer night, paradise for a couple of kids from Brooklyn was a place called Coney Island.

A few years later I learned to peddle my Columbia bicycle from Marine Park to Ocean Parkway and soon after I was on Stillwell Avenue in Coney Island. It was around that time that I became aware of Steeplechase Park, a turn-of-the-century playland that charmed my grandparents in the roaring twenties and entertained their kids during the depression. Recently, my father recalled tales of terror along the Steeplechase midway at the hands of The House of Horrors and The Castle of Death, haunted houses where children walked along dark corridors, while men dressed like mummies lurked inside shadowy doorways, eager to place a cold hand on an unsuspecting shoulder. (A recipe for a myocardial infarction if I ever heard one.)

Steeplechase Park was conceived by George Cornelius Tilyou, a visionary who began his illustrious career by selling cigar boxes, filled with "Authentic Beach Sand," to gullible tourists from the Mid-West for twenty-five cents a pop. George was a successful real-estate entrepreneur by the time he reached his mid-twenties and took his new bride to the Chicago World's Fair on their honeymoon in 1893. When Tilyou saw the first Ferris Wheel, he was so impressed that he offered to buy it on the spot and bring it back to Coney

Island. When his attempts, failed, Tilyou returned home and built his own Ferris Wheel, and several other attractions he'd seen at the World's Fair. Soon after, George's Wheel of Fortune was making more money than he had time to count, which prompted old George to begin construction on the first indoor amusement park. He called it Steeplechase, The Funny Place.

The antique amusement park vanished in 1964 and became part of Americana; however, before they paved paradise and put up a parking lot baby boomers had the opportunity to experience Steeplechase Park during the fifties and early sixties. In truth, I still have vivid memories of bright yellow buses arriving at the main entrance to Steeplechase Park just before summer break from The Good Shepherd Grammar School —the parochial school where I learned how to make the sign of the cross, while at the same time learning how to duck a *right-cross* from the good sisters.

I can still picture a flood of twelve year olds leaping from chartered buses, making a mad dash into the giant rotating barrel at the entranceway. On the other side of the spinning drum, we'd bulldoze our way through the turnstile where a group of nuns appearing more like a flock of flightless aquatic birds are giving us fair warning regarding our behavior for the next three hours. With the nuns cautionary tale in mind and our tickets in hand, we'd race through the wrought iron gates pausing briefly to absorb a cornucopia of sights and sounds. Then, my classmates and I would make a beeline for the Steeplechase stallions —the cast iron horses that galloped along steel rails encircling the entire park. Like the popular tune from *Fiddler on the Roof* riding the antique thoroughbreds, before any other attraction, was *Tradition*. Hordes of miniature city-slickers mounted the iron-steeds transforming ourselves into The Lone Ranger, Roy Rogers, and Hopalong Cassidy. Howling at the top of our lungs, "Hi-O Silver and Away" my schoolmates and I pretended to jockey for first place until our sculpted steel-champions crossed the finish line.

At the winner's circle we were ushered through a long velvety theater curtain and found ourselves center stage, chased by a clown with an electric wand zapping us to the delight of a large audience. Of course that was only the beginning of our afternoon odyssey, for off in the distance loomed a stairway that appeared to touch the clouds, a flight of steps attached to a highly-polished serpentine slide. The colossal slide was an attraction that caused more bruises and abrasions in one hour than the nuns could produce in a month. Nevertheless, I'd climb to the top of the mark and capture the attention of my pals below by posing with outstretched arms and shouting, "Top of the World Ma!" a line of dia-logue I'd recently learned from a classic

Republic film entitled *White Heat*, starring James Cagney.

In one fell swoop, I'd vanish down a narrow twisted funnel, spiraling out of control. When I popped out at the bottom of the tube, I was tossed onto revolving platters swirling in different directions and ultimately deposited on a bed of straw. Dazed and confused, I'd pick myself up, dust myself off and do it all over again. Usually after a few trips down abrasion road, I'd summon the courage it would take to experience the most dramatic plunge of all, Coney Island's main attraction: the *Parachute Jump*.

Not unlike the Parisian landmark, the Parachute Jump became Brooklyn's very own Eiffel Tower. Making its first appearance at the New York World's Fair in 1939 as an advertisement for Lifesaver Candy and later transported to Coney Island in 1941, the colossal erector-set rises two hundred and sixty-two feet above the boardwalk. Dangling precariously from wires in a floating chair with straps and buckles, while a parachute fluttered above my head, was a surreal experience. Admittedly fearful of the outcome, I'd clutch the straps on either side of the bizarre contraption until my knuckles were milky white. Soon after the parachute gradually climbed skyward and moments later, the panoramic view from aloft soothed my anxious heart.

In one direction I'd witness the island of Manhattan from Battery Park to the Empire State Building. While to the east, waves pounded the bows of majestic ocean liners and cargo ships sailing across the Atlantic. However, before I could picture a tanker's port-o-call or the Andria Doria's final destination, my parachute would reach the top and descend at what appeared to be the speed of sound. Of course it was just the speed of sound coming from my tiny voice shouting out one last time, "Top of the World Ma!" Naturally, just like my recurring slide down the twisted funnel moments later, I was once again strapped into the swaying apparatus on my way to the top.

As a child perched high atop Brooklyn's Eiffel Tower, I was invincible. Now I've re-created a posture that provides me with the tools to stay on top. Tools that give me the ability to make my dreams come true by doing the work I love. Tools that help me generate wealth from one moment to the next, fueled by imagination and conceived by common sense. The renowned women's activist Flo Kennedy once said, "Freedom is like taking a bath —you have to keep doing it every day." So I take a hot tub filled with spontaneity every day and attend to my choice voice while simple repetition adjusts my attitude and gives me the courage to dance to a different drummer. Ceaselessly I'm reminded that no one can invalidate who I am without my permission and that I alone have dominion over my dreams as long as I accept responsibility for my successes as well as my failures.

Although Steeplechase may have disappeared from Surf Avenue, it can never vanish from my heart. Within the moment, I'll ride the iron horses, slide down twisted funnels and peer out across the Atlantic. Within the moment, **sound-advice** challenges and encourages me on a ride of a lifetime, a ride that regularly swings past the fun house mirror where I glimpse a reflection that reminds me never to take myself too seriously. It's a reflection that keeps me laughing all the way to the bank.

The solution to my life
occurred to me while
I was ironing a shirt...

Alice Munro

Behind many acts that
are thought ridiculous
there lie wise and
weighty motives...

La Rochefoucauld

Cherries

In my formative years, whenever I'd get caught-up in my own drama, my mom would frequently break into song. It was a curious time to kick off a show tune, but of course there was always a method to her madness, and since mom sang like Rosemary Clooney and often attached a little soft-shoe accompaniment to her melody, I was easily distracted.

One of my mother's favorite songs was a depression era tune with lyrics that announced, "Life is just a bowl of cherries. Don't take it serious. It's too mysterious. Just keep repeating it's the berries and live and laugh at it all." I believe Bobby McFarron may have given us the modern day translation when he wrote, "Don't worry, be happy."

If memory serves, while I continued to perform the third act from Hamlet, my mother would shuffle off to Buffalo —the kitchen— where she'd attach meatball shaping and spaghetti sauce stirring to her repertoire. Naturally, my Shakespearean tragedy was doomed when mom would offer up the heel of an Italian bread dipped in spaghetti sauce. Of course by then, the unpleasantness I was experiencing would somehow vanish. I still repeat the Italian bread in the sauce routine, whether I'm feeling blue or not. The more things change, the more they remain the same.

Mom's eccentric behavior was a gift —a healthy distraction. It taught me that creating drama on stage is purposeful. However, any time I express my displeasure at something, I'm powerless to change, off stage, innocent bystanders get caught in the crossfire. My clever mother was also demonstrating that by living for the drama, instead of the comic relief, we may be unwittingly coercing people to perform in our one act play.

I'm aware that singing the blues has its place in the human condition; however, singing the blues on a daily basis, unless you're B.B. King, is a precious waste of time. Presently, I'm learning how to use the **choice concept** and **sound-advice**, whether I'm singing, "There's No Business Like Show Business," or "Am I Blue." In doing so, I'm prone to take the path of least resistance, gracefully. I may appear goofy at times, moving through life's tight spots singing and dancing, but it's a hell of a lot better than tormenting people with my own personal twaddle.

Quite a few years ago I was blessed when I read Dr. Wayne Dyer's celebrated book entitled *Your Erroneous Zones*. Dr. Dyer taught me that complaining is unhealthy and unproductive. The good doctor said that when you choose to stop complaining, you'll immediately notice how often others around you practice the useless activity. Dr. Dyer was right. I stopped. Forever.

My favorite line in the whimsical song my mother sang proclaims, "Live and laugh at it all," a notion affirming that laughter is the elixir of life. It's a philosophy I readily embrace, one that continuously allows me to examine the weight I place on ordinary life. Humor is also a shock absorber that cushions stressful situations and waves a red flag whenever anyone attempts to palm off their vapid dramatizations on me. In truth, whenever that occurs, **sound-advice** turns their passion play into the theater of the absurd. Of course if I *choose* to play the part of the town fool, that's my prerogative. In fact, it's a privilege I frequently exercise, if only to keep my ego in check —one that gives me the opportunity to bend like bamboo in the face of a storm, rather than risking self-destruction in my own rigidity.

The successful motivational speaker Cynthia Heimel said, "When in doubt, make a fool of yourself. There is a microscopically thin line between being brilliantly creative and acting like the most gigantic idiot on earth. So what the hell, leap." In reality, there are few events on God's green earth that justify serious angst, perhaps waking up in the morning and realizing that you're out of coffee might be one, slow room-service may be another. All seriousness aside, I can think of a few 'real' reasons for serious angst. However, whatever I might dish out, someone else will undoubtedly go one better, so why bother. For example, one man who tells his son he had to walk five miles to get to school every morning; however, when the next father relates the same story, he's shoeless, until ultimately someone has no feet and the last guy is likely just a head hopping along a dirt road. Cynthia's advice makes perfect sense, so I prefer to leap.

Sound-advice is a tool I use in conjunction with others I had the good fortune to acquire when I stumbled into a dimly lit college theater on a rainy Tuesday morning, more years ago than I care to remember. Holding a Styrofoam cup with black coffee in one hand, text books in the other and a bagel pressed between my teeth, I sat quietly in the balcony of the theater awaiting instructions from my first acting coach.

The imposing figure at the podium stood perfectly still waiting patiently for everyone to stop talking and take their seats. Moments later, the bustling auditorium became so quiet that one could hear a pin drop or a bite torn from a bagel in the balcony. The professor bowed his head gently and with a welcoming smile he began to teach the art of acting.

"If you take one tool away from my acting class," he said, "I hope that tool will be to recognize the moment and learn how to stay within it." I was writing the professor's first statement down when he added: "Stay in the moment and your audience will always believe in your *character*."

I didn't realize the significance or the duality of that simple statement at the time, but eventually I grew to understand his first words to his students in that beginning acting class.

He was suggesting that the thespian's physical body might be present; however, unless the actor stayed close to the moment, his intent would exit stage left long before the curtain fell on the third act. It was a fundamental principle I grasped one morning while I was doing a scene from *Death of a Salesman*, when from the back of the theater a voice announced: "Mr. Combatti, considering Willy Loman exited the theater, lets' have a picnic in Golden Gate Park. Please bring enough food for everyone, I'm afraid we all exited when Willy did." I didn't mind the joke or the sarcasm, because the professor was right on the money. I'd been *walking* through the scene rather than *working* through the scene. He was teaching me that I had to believe in my character before anyone else could. At that moment, I recognized that in order to accomplish my goals on stage, it was necessary to always be present and accounted for.

Now I not only *recognize* that the same notion holds true off stage, I *accept* that it does as well. If I remind myself to stay focused from one moment to the next, I can explore possibilities *now*, not next week, next month or next year. Similarly, if I contemplate my next move too long, the moment may be missed and my character, along with my integrity, may vanish. So I seize the opportunities I come upon every day by applying the tools I learned in college, as well as the gentle reminders I call **sound-advice**, and by doing so, I'm able to champion my own destiny.

I rehearse the concepts of choice and **sound-advice**, the same way the good professor taught me to rehearse lines for a play. Once again, repetition rules the day, prompting me to recall again and again that I always have a choice. They are simple admonitions that adjust my attitude, lift my spirit and improve my disposition. So if you happen to hear someone doing a wacky rendition of *Life is Just a Bowl of Cherries* while they're purchasing a pound of coffee or a pair of running shoes, introduce yourself. Who knows, we may end up doing a little harmony, and if my wife is cooking Italian, I'll turn you on to a chunk of Italian bread dipped in spaghetti sauce.

Life is a stage, and
we are all merely
players...

William Shakespeare

The obscure we see eventually, the completely apparent takes longer...

Edward R. Murrow

A Gypsy Cried

I was thirteen years old when I first met Marty Selzer. Marty was tough, smart, and good looking, a triple threat that had every girl in the neighborhood vying for the opportunity to see her name at the top of the charts. Naturally, *Marty's Girl* became the song title quite a few young ladies had occasion to sing.

Marty lived on East 59th Street, just across the street from my Uncle Vic and Aunt Lucille, neatly tucked away in a corner of Brooklyn called Mill Basin. The Basin, as we called it, was a community of middle-class homes and shops just beyond the reaches of Brownsville and East New York, although not quite far enough away from the outstretched arms of Canarsie.

In the fifties, the Basin was a huge playground with farms and ranches and riding academies with horses that galloped along the beaches. In the fifties, the Basin had wide open spaces for kids to run around and explore, acres of fresh land and untapped real estate. It was an expanse of undeveloped

Brooklyn my relatives discovered long before the population on every borough exploded. Nowadays, in order to explore untapped land in New York, you may have to travel a little further. I imagine ninety miles north of Peeksville might be a good jumping off point.

Just after my aunt and uncle bought their new home, my parents decided to take the plunge, purchasing a three bedroom townhouse in the Marine Park section of Brooklyn. It was a quaint neighborhood with tall oak trees fashioning a canopy from one side of East 29th Street to the other. Our new home was only a short walk to Sheepshead Bay, and just a stone's throw from Vic and Lucille —a turn of events that brought *la familia* closer and gave my sister and I more opportunities to play with our cousins and their friends.

When I first met my cousin Eddie's two friends, Marty and Bobby, they treated me like one of the usual suspects. Cousin or no cousin, I lived in a different part of town, and kids from New York —like kids everywhere— are territorial. So, it was touch and go for a while until I demonstrated my worthiness —a feat I accomplished by using my rapier wit, charming personality and dazzling footwork. In truth, I still win friends and influence people the same way, although my fancy footwork may be a little rusty.

Naturally with my approval rating on the rise, whenever my folks were visiting my aunt and uncle, I'd call on Marty and Bobby. Then, we'd roam the neighborhood from Floyd Bennett Field to the *Circle G Stables*, a ramshackle horse-for-hire outfit, complete with urban cowboys running the operation, while tenderfoots (my pals and I) ran amuck. As closely as I can determine, every trip we ever made to the rusting red barn had the same primary objective —to sing the praises of *Have Gun Will Travel* a few hundred times until the owners firmly, but politely, suggested we take our boots and our business elsewhere. In truth, our little side trips to the Circle G instilled a lifelong appreciation for the mighty stead. As a matter of course, I still know more about the care and grooming of horses than I do about rotating the tires on my car. In fact, some years later I landed a terrific summer job, driving a horse and carriage in Central Park, so *Have Gun Will Travel* rocked on. However, long before I crisscrossed Central Park in a horse and buggy, I still needed my parents permission to crisscross Marine Park on my bicycle. So I poured on the charm and the fancy footwork, and soon after, I officially became one of the *59th Street Boys*. And about the same time, Marty and Bobby became part of my extended family.

Bobby was a chubby hot-headed kid with a good heart and an even better sense of humor, while Marty was a level-headed lad with a noble demeanor, and without question the funniest kid in our company of players. At first we weren't certain why Marty was so funny, but we soon learned that it wasn't *what* he said, but rather *how* he said it that made us laugh. At the tender age of thirteen, Marty was becoming the master of the understatement, casually saying something offbeat, then pretending that he didn't understand why we were laughing, which of course only made us laugh even harder. In the humor arena, Bobby and I were generally over the top —slapstick city. A phenomenon which frequently meant that wherever the three of us were, the motion picture event: *Abbot and Costello, Meet Steven Wright* got two thumbs up. Not unlike Charles Dickens' opening line in *A Tale of Two Cities*, "It was the best of times..."

In a New York minute, pages were flying off the calendar like some old movie, and my high school principal William "Wild Bill" Friedman was shaking hands and handing out diplomas. Soon after, baby boomers either marched off to war or became the next generation of the working proletariat. My little crew managed to fall into the latter arrangement. Luckily, we all slipped through the cracks of the giant war machine; however, now it was time to step up to the plate and make our mark in the world. Bobby went into the banking business first, while Marty got a job with a brokerage firm somewhere in lower Manhattan. I, of course, dreamed of a viable alternative to the nine to five affliction: show business.

Unfortunately, my parents and I weren't on the same page. So, I enrolled in an eight week course in computer technology at a business school in midtown Manhattan —a daunting task, considering computers in the sixties were about the size of an eight-bedroom house. Nevertheless, I did the deed and received my crash-course certificate with honors, which was pretty amusing, considering I knew less about computers when I completed the course than when I'd started. Nevertheless, I began applying for work on Wall Street, and three days later Dean Witter & Company got lucky.

After a brief orientation on my first day of work, my immediate supervisor, a droll Jamaican import by the name of Winston Leeds, escorted me along a maze of corridors with plush carpets and textured walls. When we arrived in front of a pair of giant oak doors with gold lettering that read *Dean Witter & Company*, Winston (as he preferred to be called) paused briefly before turning the doorknob. Then, in a classic Jamaican accent and a broad smile, Winston announced: "Don't look so scary, Mr. Michael. It's only a job." (**Sound-advice** I frequently used over the years.) Then, in one fell swoop, the door was open and I stepped across the threshold. On the other side of the portal was a sweeping office crowded with whirring machines, buzzing key punch operators, and giant computers. Call it karma, destiny, or just a simple twist of fate, but the first face I saw when I walked through the door was my friend Marty Selzer. There are ten million people in New York City and a billion places to work, and just a few weeks earlier Marty had landed a job with the same company. The odds of that occurring are astronomical. Finding a winning lottery ticket stuck to the bottom of your shoe might be a close second.

When I walked through the double doors, the look on Marty's face was priceless. For a split second, my friend thought I'd spoken to his mom, found out where he worked, and was bombing in on him for lunch. Smiling from ear to ear, Marty quickly came over and told Winston that he and I were friends. Although he'd only been with the brokerage firm a short time, Winston asked him to show me the ropes, and I was off and running. Naturally, my friend made the awkward feeling that accompanies the first day on the job appear as though it didn't exist. Together, we were a couple of kids discovering the burgeoning computer industry on the seventeenth floor of an imposing building simply labeled *Two Broadway*.

The next three years at Dean Witter & Company were pure dynamite. Each day I'd travel into Manhattan via the subway and exit at the Bowling Green Station. Then, I'd climb the waffled iron staircase, shoulder to shoulder with the rank and file of the greatest city in the world. Once inside the polished limestone lobby, I'd stand in front of a gang of elevators, surrounded by a swarm of my fellow worker bees, while one by one we'd glance at our wrist watches, anxiously waiting to be lifted above the sidewalks of New York into a building that scraped the sky.

When I arrived on seventeen, I'd stand along a row of windows with a cup of java in one hand and a briefcase in the other. High above the madding crowd, I'd watch the ferries gliding across the bay, frequently docking alongside the Statue of Liberty and Ellis Island, the island where my ancestors disembarked at the turn of the century, carrying cardboard suitcases filled with dreams — hearty people who sailed on powerful steamships with names like Ancona and the SS Vincenzo Florio, arriving from countries where Roman empires once ruled and the Emerald Isle to the north. Then, after I viewed the performance on the Hudson Bay and surveyed the bottom of my coffee cup, it was business as usual.

When Bobby learned that Citibank, located on the main floor of Two Broadway, was hiring, he immediately applied for a job. Three days later, my best friends and I were all working in the same building, which meant that sharing lunch in Battery Park would soon become a daily ritual. Of course, in those days, our lunch consisted of a Sabrette hot dog and a couple of tokes on the old peace pipe, or a peanut butter and jelly sandwich and a couple of tokes on the old peace pipe, or a slice of pizza and a... Well, you get the picture. Naturally, after passing the grass around, we'd laugh our asses off for the next forty-five minutes until it was time to head back to the salt mines. Then, Bobby would return to Citibank while Marty and I waited for the next available elevator to the 17th floor. When the elevator arrived, Marty and I would step to the rear of the car and avoid looking at one another at all costs, knowing only too well that one passing glance could cause a chain reaction of laughter. Our spontaneous laughter was an involuntary reflex. One that commonly occurred whenever the elevator was crammed with co-workers or if we were standing behind the company's corporate executive, Billy Reitz.

Billy was the head honcho on the 17th floor, the man with the power to amplify your paycheck or tell you to hit the bricks. A decent chap in his late fifties, Billy stood about four feet eleven in his stocking feet and sported the best swoop-over hairstyle in New York City. He also had a high-pitched voice that sounded somewhat constricted. I used to say that Billy's comb-over made him look like an iguana with a perm. Marty maintained that whenever Billy spoke, it sounded like someone was trying to strangle him. Of course, the mere thought of either of those observations could make our trip to the 17th floor feel like an eternity.

When the elevator doors opened on seventeen, my friend and I would take a deep breath, step lively and make our way down the hall. However, before we could make a clean getaway, Mr. Reitz would frequently turn on his heels and say, "Lunch in the park again, ay fellas? The grass couldn't be greener, whad'ya say?" Naturally, we couldn't say anything, at least not coherently. So we'd just stand there grinning like a couple of boneheads, until Mr. Reitz disappeared through the large oak doors. Then, for the remainder of the day Marty and I would ponder Billy's choice of words. Perhaps a casual remark to the rest of the employees, but to my friend and I, Billy's comment sounded like a mixed metaphor. We were convinced that Mr. Reitz was actually saying, "Great day to smoke some weed, ay fellas!?" Paranoid? Oh, maybe a tad. Nevertheless, Marty and I loved to question Billy's purity of heart, theorizing that Dean Witter's very own corporate munchkin may have been enjoying a toke or two on his own peace pipe. After all, it was the sixties, and everyone appeared to be doing a little "research." Even future presidents were experimenting with *Cannabis*, although of course they weren't "inhaling."

My days at Dean Witter & Company were filled with colorful chapters in a book I wouldn't alter for a king's ransom. It was a time when I began to grasp the true meaning of the word "bonding," a genuine connection that may only occur once in a lifetime. While a great many friendships are fleeting at best, when I pause to reflect on that time in my life, I'm mindful that true friendship is a difficult commodity to acquire.

Three years later, once again the pages from the calendar were floating on the wind, and Dean Witter and I were going our separate ways. I was embarking on a journey to follow my dream, and this time computer technology wasn't part of my trek. Soon after, Bobby left Citibank for bigger and better banks, while Marty worked his way up the corporate ladder at Two Broadway. In the interim, Marty had an office romance, got married with a child on the way, and moved across the Verrazano Bridge. The only drawback to this storybook scenario was that Marty's running buddies seldom got to see his smiling face except on that rare occasion when, after visiting his mom, he'd drive past our old hangout on Ralph Avenue, which is where I caught up to him one balmy summer night in August of nineteen hundred and sixty-nine.

I'd just driven into the parking lot of the Gil Hodges Bowling Alley when I saw Marty turn the corner in his new Mustang. I hopped out of my car and waved, and Marty smiled and waved back. When the traffic light on Ralph Avenue turned green, Marty made a quick U-turn and drove back to the bowling alley. He pulled into the empty space alongside my Triumph, leaned over the console and cranked down the passenger window. Marty asked me if I wanted to take a spin out to Rockaway. Without uttering a word, I opened the door to Marty's Mustang and hopped in —a minute later, we were down the road burnin' gas.

During the summer months, my friends and I often drove out to Rockaway, just for something to do. It was only a short ride to Rockaway Playland, an amusement park we visited when we needed a Coney Island fix but weren't up to dealing with the urban blight along Stillwell Avenue. In addition, waves crashing on the shore were always a welcome change from listening to the pins colliding at the bowling alley.

Cruising out to Rockaway in Marty's new Mustang was a rush. His eight track stereo was cranked up and the windows were cranked down. The summer wind was blowing cool, while the Rolling Stones were having their *Nineteenth Nervous Breakdown*, and Marty and I were helping Mick and the boys hit the high notes. We were on a magic carpet ride, bounding across the Riis Park Bridge, laughing and talking about everyone at Dean Witter & Company, especially our old boss, Billy Reitz. While Marty focused on the road, I turned away for a couple of seconds, and when I turned back I'd combed my hair over to one side and made myself small. Then, while I moved my lips, Marty did a vocal impression of Billy that knocked my socks off. Using Billy's key expressions, Marty made Mr. Reitz sound like a cross between Ed Sullivan and Kermit the Frog. We called the character *Kermit Sullivan*. Of course the first line Marty had our old boss say, was: "Lunch in the park again, ay fellas?" followed by, "The 'grass' couldn't be greener, whad'ya say?" Then, Marty kicked it up a notch: "Do you fellas know where I can score some good weed, Maryjane, Black Gunja, whad'ya say?" Marty was on a roll, steering with one hand and pretending to strangle himself with the other. When we finished our little skit, I was on the floorboards and my buddy was in tears. Then, just five minutes down the pike, we were cruising along Beach Channel Drive, approaching the cool winds that reach across the Atlantic and the sights and sounds of Rockaway Playland.

When we arrived on Rockaway Blvd and 98th Street, it appeared as though half the population of New York City had had the same idea. As a result, Marty and I drove around for quite a stretch, until we spied a parking spot in front of a small shop with a neon sign above the door that read *Psychic Reader*. The little shop with the neon sign had been converted into a quasi living room, complete with sofa, overstuffed chair and a tall lamp. Along the sidewalk, an elderly woman wearing a peasant blouse and a long brown skirt, donning more jewelry than Joan Rivers sells in a month on QVC, sat stoically at a small card table near the curb. While Marty was backing into the parking space, the gypsy kept repeating in a thick slavic accent, "See the future, young men. It's only a dollar to see the future." She reminded me of Maria Ouspenskaya, the tiny Russian actress with the beady eyes in the classic film *The Wolfman*. I thought that any moment she might proclaim: "I see on your hand you have the mark of the pentagram!"

About that time, I turned toward Marty and quietly said, "She's a little scary. Besides, if she can see the future, why is she living in a storefront near an amusement park?" If nothing else she was persistent, so I smiled politely and thanked her. I'm sure I had other things on my mind that evening, like going in search of Miss Right, or at least Miss Right Now. And if a female wasn't in the cards, I'd console myself with a beer and a slice of pizza.

The parking space was a bear, but Marty did the deed and we were in like Flynn. However, before we were able to slip past our tenacious friend, the old woman gave it one last shot. Marty and I smiled at the fortune-teller, then turned toward the bright lights and the sound of the roller coaster clacking in the distance. However, before I could take another step in the direction of the Atom Smasher or the House of Horrors, Marty placed his hand on my shoulder and asked me to hold up for a second. He said that he wanted to check it out. I turned toward my friend with a pointed grin and said, "Check what out?" and Marty replied, "The future."

At first I thought he was kidding, but he wasn't. To begin with, I found it difficult to understand why Marty was willing to spend a perfectly good dollar to hear some meaningless crap. In the sixties, a buck bought a slice of pizza and a cold one, and you'd still have enough money left over for a gallon of gas. However, my friend was determined to have his fortune told. So, he sat down at the table across from the gypsy and handed her a dollar. The gypsy took the money and Marty's hand at the same time, while I stood behind my friend, looking across the table at Madam Zorina. In truth, I don't recall the fortune-teller's name, but whatever she was calling herself that night, my friend Marty was buying.

We were all smiling when Marty sat down, but the mood quickly changed. The fortune-teller held his hand, but never looked at it. Instead, she gazed directly into Marty's eyes and immediately became distressed.

At once, her countenance appeared sorrowful yet frightened. Then she said, "I see something very, very bad."

I nearly laughed out loud. If that didn't sound like a line of musty dialogue from *The Curse of the Werewolf*, I'd never heard one. I thought surely Marty would glance over his shoulder with an expression that said, "What a load of crap." However, he never looked away from the gypsy's gaze, and continued to stare across the table.

What followed next was extremely uncharacteristic for anyone in that line of work. "I'm very sorry, young man; please, I'm very sorry." She continued, "This is very bad." About this time, things began to get positively hinky. The elderly woman looked up at me and I could see that she was trembling. When she looked back at Marty, she said, "Take your money back, please take it back!" I can hear her voice wavering as if it were yesterday, repeating again and again, "Take your money back, young man, please take it back!"

Granted, I'm not an authority on Bohemian folklore; however, I can say with a certain amount of confidence that gypsies *never* give *anyone* their money back. I think it's safe to say that it's against their religion, considering the almighty dollar is likely a psychic's only god. Nevertheless, the gypsy insisted that he take his money back, pushing the crumpled dollar across the table, until Marty finally took it from her hand. A moment later, she slowly got up from her chair and stepped back from the table, while everything on the street seemed to fall silent. At last, Marty turned in his chair and peered over his shoulder. He looked uncomfortable and more than a little embarrassed. I responded by flashing Marty my overworked "forgetaboutit" smirk, a facial cast that said the entire event was stupid and not worth a second thought. Although in truth, I thought the whole experience was damned unpleasant.

During the gypsy's little fiasco, I'd had my hand on the back of Marty's folding chair. So, when he began to get up, I pulled the metal chair along the sidewalk, making it easy for him to step away from the table. When I glanced at Marty's face again —anticipating the same uncomfortable expression— I saw something very different. Standing motionless on the sidewalk, Marty looked peaceful and perhaps a little sad. His demeanor appeared calm and untroubled. He still hadn't moved, standing there rigid with his arms down by his sides, staring off into space. I thought for a second I might have to shake him by the shoulders and shout, "Snap out of it!" Instead, I just tapped his arm with the back of my hand, and motioned with my eyes and a slight tilt of my head that it was time for us to take our leave. As we turned to walk away, Marty paused on the sidewalk to put the dollar bill back in his wallet. Then, he took one last look over his shoulder, but our soothsayer had already gone through the beaded doorway and into the makeshift living room.

Once again, Marty and I were walking toward the sound of the wooden roller coaster creeping up a steep grade, while off in the distance I could hear a faint measure of music from a calliope. Although somehow, now, everything sounded eerily out of place. Nearly halfway down the block, neither of us had said a word.

Then, when the silence was about to become deafening, I finally said, "The next time you wanna check out the future..." But before I could finish the sentence, Marty added, "I know, I'll give you a dollar and you'll call me in the morning."

Then, just as if we'd been rehearsing a powerful do-wop falsetto, that even Frankie Valli would have applauded, we began singing, *The Gypsy Cried*. We were laughing, but undeniably the mood that night had shifted. I felt as though something dark was hanging in the air. Some *thing* that made me feel a little empty.

We continued down the street to an Irish pub on the corner and ordered a beer at the bar. Neither of us said a word about the gypsy, instead we talked about the recent moon landing everyone was buzzing about and the concert I was looking forward to attending in upstate New York. Marty was a little disappointed that he wouldn't be able to go to the concert. Of course, he had no way of knowing about the three days of mud, music and mayhem the festival promoters had in store for me, and that although I'd enjoy seeing Jimi Hendrix and Janis Joplin, the only way I'd ever take part in another concert with five-hundred thousand people would be if I were kidnapped and hurled into the festival from the Goodyear Blimp. In passing, I said that the couple I was going to Woodstock with were taking their two year old daughter along. I asked Marty if he'd ever consider taking his kid to a Woodstock-type extravaganza. At first, there was an awkward silence.

Then Marty took a long sip from his beer and finally said, "I don't think I'll be around long enough to find out." I said that that was a wacky thing to say, but Marty just shrugged his shoulders and changed the subject.

Our trip back to Mill Basin was a lot different from our jaunt out to Rockaway. Marty's eight track was silent, and so was he. I was certain my friend was reflecting on the bizarre behavior of the black forest doomsayer earlier that evening. However, I thought it was best to let that riddle fade into the night. So we sat there in silence, and twenty minutes later we were back where we began.

Before I could open the door to Marty's Mustang, he turned to me and said that he was glad that I'd waved at him and gotten his attention. He said that it was fun tripping out to Rockaway Playland. I told Marty that it was good to see his smiling face too. I said that I was glad he'd decided to take a swing past the bowling alley. Then I hopped out, walked around to the driver's side window, touched Marty's arm and said, "I'll talk to you soon." But it wasn't soon enough, because three days later Marty Selzer died of a massive heart attack at the age of twenty-two.

When the phone rang, I immediately recognized Mike Casillo's voice. Mike and I had
become friends shortly before I left Dean
Witter & Co. Without hesitation, Mike said,
"Michael, I've got really bad news. Marty
Selzer died." I paused for a second and said,
"That's not funny." But of course it wasn't a
joke. I sat on the corner of my bed and asked
Mike how Marty had died. He told me that my
childhood friend had died of heart failure. He
knew that Marty and I had been friends since
we were kids and said he was sorry for my
loss. I thanked Mike for calling and said I'd
touch base later that evening. Of course, I
immediately called Bobby, but the line was
busy. Then, just as I was placing the receiver
back in the cradle, the phone rang out —it
was Bobby. I told him that I'd just heard the
tragic news. Bobby was trying to give me the
details surrounding Marty's death, but he was
having a difficult time doing so. He'd begin to
speak, than he'd pause, unable to finish every
sentence. "Marty's gone man.... his heart.... I
don't know. He had a history.... a serious
problem..... he's gone, Mikie....Marty's gone."
Bobby struggled to tell me about the ambu-
lance and how the paramedics couldn't find
Marty's address. My head was spinning and
everything sounded jumbled. I slid off the
side of the bed and sat on the floor. Then I
heard Bobby say, "Over thirty minutes had
passed, can you believe it... *thirty minutes...* by
that time, he was gone."

It took some time before I was able to accept that Marty was no longer with us. When his death appeared too real, I'd switch to a comfortable state of denial, as if at any minute he was going to pop up at the bowling alley and we'd take a ride out to Rockaway, or cruise over to Coney Island for a hot dog at Nathan's. None of it made any sense. Although, I finally understood why people often say, "I want to go to sleep, and tomorrow when I wake up, this ordeal may only be a bad dream." Of course, the following morning I woke up to another day, but Marty never would.

Bobby was devastated by Marty's death. At the wake, Bobby sat in the back of the funeral parlor for hours, motionless. Just recently engaged with the celebration only months away, Bobby's best man had suddenly died. When he did speak, Bobby kept repeating that this wasn't the way things were supposed to be. I've often thought that Bobby never fully recovered from Marty's untimely death, that there would always be a feeling of abandonment; a void that could never be filled.

When I left the funeral parlor, I put the top down on my convertible and drove around for hours. Without intentionally driving out to Rockaway, I somehow landed on the beach near the amusement park. In the distance, I could here faint screams emanating from the roller coaster and the sound of the calliope

Marty and I listened to just a few days earlier. I thought about the gypsy and pondered if she was sitting at the little folding table on the sidewalk. Although, I didn't care to find out. Instead, I continued to sit near the edge of the water, listening to the waves pounding the shoreline and staring at the Atlantic. I was a tough kid from the streets and wouldn't allow anyone to witness my pain, so I cried in the dark and fell asleep on the sand. It was nearly dawn when I woke up, chilled to the bone. I brushed the sand from my hair and drove back to my apartment in South Brooklyn.

The entire time I'd known Marty Selzer, he'd never mentioned that as a child he was extremely ill, and that as a result of that illness, he'd developed a heart problem. Marty desperately needed an operation, but he knew that bypass procedures were still experimental, and that only a small percentage of the patients who underwent them survived. Consequently, with no visible signs of disease, Marty was reluctant to accept the counsel of his physicians. In fact, the same day he and I had driven out to Rockaway, he'd postponed his pre-arranged admission to the hospital.

Some people believe that Marty was playing a dangerous waiting game, but I was never comfortable with that theory. I believe my friend may have chosen another path, one where he'd come to terms with his own mortality, reasoning that it would be pointless to spend his last days on earth grasping at straws when he could be enjoying life, in the moment, hitting the high notes. Of course, I'll never really know the truth. Although there is one truth I'll always embrace: on a balmy summer night over thirty years ago, an old gypsy woman peered into my friend's soul and witnessed the end of a journey. That journey may have been short, but it was teeming with kindness, humor and always mindful of the moment. My friend Marty was as pleasant a young man as anyone could ever imagine, lighting up rooms wherever he went and putting smiles on the faces of everyone he encountered. He was clearly one of a kind, and I'll always miss him.

A few years back, I had a vivid dream about my childhood friend. I was sitting on an aisle seat in a crowded movie theater. The film was about to begin, when suddenly someone placed their hand on my shoulder. When I looked back, Marty was standing off to my right. He looked the way he had the night he and I cruised out to Rockaway. His face was beaming, and the hand he placed on my shoulder felt the way it had when he paused on the sidewalk that summer night, announcing that he wanted to see the future.

I sat there for a few seconds, smiling and looking up at my friend, until at last I said, "It's great to see you."

Marty squeezed my shoulder a little and then he said, "It's good to see you too."

I said, "We all miss you. How long can you stay?"

"I can't stay long," he said. "I just came to tell you I'm doing well."

I was about to stand up when Marty gestured toward the silver screen. I turned to look at the film and Marty was gone. I wish I could say that when I looked toward the screen, Frank Capra's classic film *It's a Wonderful Life* was playing, or *Heaven Can Wait*, but the truth is, I can't recall what movie was playing, and shortly thereafter I awoke.

My dream didn't have a spectacular ending or great visual effects; however, it did come with an innocent wake-up call, one that announced that my friend would be there for me, forever. Sharp images of a young man who may have heard the sound of his own voice whispering in the wind.

Marty understood the **choice concept** and **sound-advice** on several different levels. He not only lived in the moment, he also allowed any individual who was fortunate enough to be in his presence, the power to experience their very own personal brand of freedom. He chose humor as his vehicle to arrive at a comfortable place to exchange ideas —leading his audience down one path, then changing his course at the last minute, to reach a destination that brought about laughter.

Frequently, I listen to a choice-voice that reminds me to live each day like my good hearted friend Martin. It's a choice-voice that reminds me to exercise a generous nature, while reminding me, continuously, that *life* is clearly a *gift*. My choice-voice is an extension of the **sound-advice** I use from one moment to another —sound vibrations that remind me that life is fleeting, precious and not permanent.

At the tender age of twenty-two, my friend Marty understood what the renowned author Ursula K. LeGuin proclaimed so eloquently, when she said, "It is good to have an end to journey towards; but it is the journey that matters, in the end."

Quit now, you'll never make it. If you disregard this advice, you'll be half-way there...

David Zuker

In Conclusion

While I was writing this book, whenever anyone asked me what it was about I'd say, "It's about a hundred and fifty pages." When the groaning died down, I'd often say that the book was a compilation of short stories about not taking life too seriously, because it isn't permanent. I'd add that I had suddenly understood something I'd known all along, only in a new way and that I wanted to tell people about it. However, most importantly this book was about a journey; a trek that continues to allow me to adjust my attitude from one moment to the next. I turned a major corner in my life while I was writing this book and I hope you'll do some major corner turning as well. I'd also like to take a moment to thank the audience members I shamelessly disarmed, while I was putting my thoughts down on paper. Thanks for the laughs.

Always leave 'em
laughin'.

About the Author

Michael Combatti likes to say that he hails from the south "South Brooklyn." He grew up in the 50s and 60s only a short distance from Coney Island. In the mid seventies, after working on Wall Street for several years, Michael took Horace Greeley's advice and went west. He arrived on the U.C. Berkeley campus in 1973 and soon after began calling California his home. He studied media communication and theater arts for several years; however, in the midst of the stand up comedy craze, he took to the stage. Soon after, he became a permanent fixture on the San Francisco and Los Angeles Comedy club circuit. While studying the art of acting and improvisation in Berkeley and later in Los Angeles, he became fascinated with eastern philosophy and the psychology of humor. His passion for exploring the human condition while criss-crossing America as a stand-up comedian, blossomed into a genuine strategy for positive change; a simple system he reveals through a compilation of funny and often touching short stories. As an actor Michael has been privileged to work with Academy Award winner Tom Hanks, as well as Sally Fields and Diane Keaton. When he isn't writing, acting, or on the road doing stand-up comedy, Michael can be found playing the piano for his family, or wailing on his blues harmonica, in one of the many clubs surrounding San Francisco. Michael Combatti listens closely to sound-advice and truly lives in the moment.